ANNIE SLOAN'S
PAINTED KITCHEN

ANNIE SLOAN'S
PAINTED KITCHEN

paint effect transformations for walls, cupboards, and furniture

Annie Sloan

LAUREL
GLEN

San Diego, California

Laurel Glen Publishing

An imprint of the Advantage Publishers Group

5880 Oberlin Drive, San Diego, CA 92121-4794

www.laurelglenbooks.com

All notations of errors or omissions should be addressed
to Laurel Glen Publishing, Editorial Department, at the
above address. All other correspondence (author
inquiries, permissions, and rights) concerning the
content of this book should be addressed to Cico Books
Ltd, 32 Great Sutton Street, London, UK, EC1V 0NB.

ISBN 1-59223-184-5
Library of Congress Cataloging-in-Publication Data
available upon request.

Printed in China

1 2 3 4 5 08 07 06 05 04

Editor: Robin Gurdon
Designer: Jonathan Raimes
Photographer: Tino Tedaldi

contents

introduction: the painted kitchen

Every kitchen should have a character. Some are sleek and cool, while others are comfy and comical. There are large farmhouse-style kitchens and tiny galley kitchens. Kitchens can be based on a French style, Africa, or any period, country, or theme you want.

The kitchen used to be the domain of women, where only cooking, washing dishes, and the laundry were done. Now, more and more, kitchens are the hub of the home, where friends and family congregate at the end of the day. There is likely to be a table that will be used for both eating and perhaps hobbies and paperwork, and there may even be a sofa and a television. The dining room, the study, and the sitting room have entered the kitchen. Consult my Inspirations pages that run throughout the book to help you decide on the style of kitchen that suits you best. Bear in mind that kitchens are a comfort zone, not only purely functional, but can easily feast the eye as well as the taste buds.

The choice of kitchen color has broadened. White, green, and blue are traditional, but in recent years the rich earth tones of Africa, as well as reds and pinks, have become fashionable. All the paints featured in the book are from the Annie Sloan range, and many come in practical, hard-wearing finishes. For expert tips on how to match your own favorite colors with the best complementary colors, consult the colorboards throughout the book—from picking a series of hot fuschia swatches in the Pink Kitchen to the cool neutral color combinations shown in the Modern Kitchen.

Kitchen furniture has also changed. We now not only use built-in, purpose-built kitchen units, but also reclaim old pieces of furniture from the junkyard. More and more people have free-standing pieces, or import thrift-store finds, for an individual look. And as new paints, coverings, and equipment appear on the market, we can now transform off-the-shelf kitchens and worn wooden or melamine units with very little expense, in a startlingly short time. For a truly personal finish, paint is the best way to change the way your kitchen looks, whether you use it on the units, on the walls, or both. Shown in the first chapters of this book, the tools and techniques that you need are simple to use. You will find paints and finishes for every look you need, including glitter, metallics, and pearly paints, as well as papers and foils. Plain or distressed, gilded or foiled, stenciled, or découpaged, simple paint effects can be completely transforming and each will be, of course, unique to you and your home.

Once you have chosen a theme and the colors of your kitchen, you can work through the projects you need. Within each style of kitchen is a series of projects I created on site as well as extra projects that suit the look you choose to create. Always remember that most of the twenty-five projects can be done in a variety of colors, and that, as you become more adventurous, you can use the technical guidance throughout the book to mix and match your own effects and finishes.

materials
and tools

gilding & foiling

fine wire wool
Grade 0000, used for applying wax over leaf to age and distress it

soft-haired brush
To stick the leaf to the base

fine varnish brush
To apply the gold size

There are two main types of gilding materials available—leaf and foil. Both are applied to a base surface using the same basic method with a glue called gold size. The newer material, metallic foil, is available in long rolls, one side of which is shiny and metallic while the reverse has a cream-colored, matte finish. The foil is much shinier than the leaf, has a modern look, and does not tarnish.

The leaf is real metal pressed extremely thinly into 5 inch squares. They are bought in bound books made up of tissue paper with a leaf of metal slid between each tissue sheet.

gold size
The glue for applying leaf and metallic foil

dark and clear wax
Used to help age and distress the leaf

metallic foil
Various metal effects, such as copper, bright and dull gold, silver, pewter, and champagne silver; available in 2-foot-long rolls

loose-leaf foil
Available in copper, brass, and aluminum, twenty-five sheets in each book

sponge roller
For applying base coats and paint in stripes

spotty roller
Rubber roller for making spots on the wall

mutton cloth
For cloudy effects

large house painting brush
Ideal for color washing

dragging brush and paintbrush
Various sizes to apply paint to furniture and for glaze painting

color washing & distressing

The water-based, scumble glaze is the most important material needed. Developed hundreds of years ago by artists wanting to imitate wood graining and marble, it is used in every color-washing technique to give depth to the color and allow you to work the paint freely until you have the look you want. The glaze is usually applied with a cloth, though all sorts of combs and short-haired brushes can be used to make specific effects.

When distressing, the look that is being emulated is of old furniture. Nowadays water-based paints that will absorb wax are used to create the look of old paintwork. The wax will give it the sheen of old oil paint and will also help break down the paint to make it look scratched and gently worn. Having the right paint will certainly aid the quality of your work. Always have a few different qualities of sandpaper—coarse and very fine—so you can vary the amount of distressing.

clear wax
For applying to chalk paint to help it soften so it will be easy to distress it

water-based paint
To mix with glaze

water-based glaze
Although it looks white, it will dry clear

sandpaper
Various grades to rub off the waxed paint

mosaic & découpage

In making a mosaic design, you can utilize the small conventional tiles for mosaics as well as old tiles and plates. For decorating furniture by making a border rather than as a true mosaic, the tiles only need to be glued down and not grouted.

glue

mosaic tiles

tile cutters

gift wrap

high-build découpage
varnish

varnish brush

Wrapping papers are one of the easiest
ways of finding designs for découpage,
and there are many varieties available.
Other methods of getting images
include scanning pictures into a
computer—this also allows you to
flip or enlarge the design. This way,
family photographs can be used
without ruining the original.

sharp scissors

acetate stencil

sponge
Ordinary household sponges can be cut into shapes for printing. Draw on them first with a pen to act as a guide.

scissors
A really sharp and pointed pair of scissors is a must.

stenciling & printing

These are both methods of making patterns on walls and furniture. They are a great way to paint if you lack the confidence to work freehand.

There are many ready-made stencils available covering all types and styles of decoration, from the medieval—as seen here—to the modern. You can make your own stencils, too, which involves using a sharp knife or a hot cutting knife.

You can buy ready-made stamps in a variety of designs or you can make your own using sponges or potatoes.

roller tray and small roller
For applying paint to stencils

roller
For applying paint to stencils

water-based paint

brush
For applying paint to stamps

cover potato with water-based paint

the techniques

gilding

Traditional leaf is real metal and is bought in tissue paper books holding twenty-five leaves. Being real metal, the copper and brass leaf tarnishes unless it is protected from air to stop it from oxidizing. This is done with varnish or wax. The result is a traditional look.

1 Choose a color for the base of the gilding to contrast or complement the metallic color. Allow to dry.

2 Apply a coat of gold size thoroughly, but not too thickly. It will be purplish white at first before drying clear. When it is clear it is ready to use.

3 Gently drop the square of leaf on the surface of the size. Once it touches, it will stick. Brush out the leaf with a soft but firm brush so it adheres completely and evenly. Dust your hands lightly with talcum powder if the leaf is sticking to them.

metallic foil

Despite its name, metallic foil is not real metal. Its advantage is that it will not tarnish, but, because it is so bright, it suits a more modern look. Follow the first two steps of the gilding process and then apply the foil. Also remember that there is a right side and a wrong side.

4 Subsequent pieces can be added easily and any gaps can be repaired if you want a completely covered look.

5 Apply the foil with the shiny side up. Rub firmly with your hand and test to see how much of the metal finish has come off. If you need to apply more pressure, try using a brush.

6 Pull off the thin plastic backing to leave the foil sticking to the size.

color washing

Color washing has become the generic word for all the techniques that use scumble glaze or, as it is sometimes known, transparent glaze. With the basic mixture you can do many techniques such as color washing, dragging, combing, and clouding with a piece of mutton cloth. All these techniques have a long history but it is the colors and the combinations that give them a modern look.

The purpose of the glaze is to make the paint translucent, and to help the paint dry slowly while you wipe it and dab it with your cloth, comb, or brush.

the basic mixture

This is the same for all the glazing techniques, being a mixture of transparent glaze and paint. The exact ratios depend on how opaque you want the mixture to be (add more paint for a more opaque mixture).

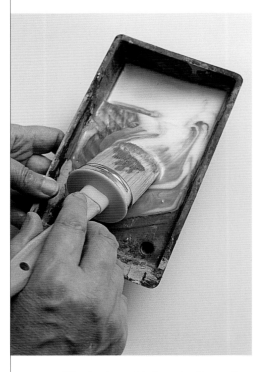

1 Mix the glaze with the paint. First make a mixture in a small roller tray and when you are sure of your color make a larger amount in a pail so you have enough for the entire job.

2 Brush the glaze onto the surface, making certain you can see the base color through the colored glaze. Do not apply it too thickly, but give a thorough coat. You are now ready to do any of the other finishes.

mutton cloth

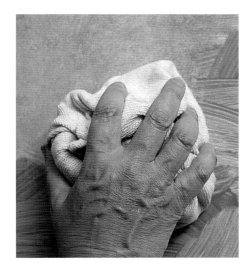

1 Apply the glaze so it is fairly generous. Make sure that the cloth's ends are folded in making a ball shape out of the fabric so that it can be bounced and dabbed off the surface.

2 Alternatively, use a cloth to wipe off the paint going in all directions, leaving a wet edge to join the next section.

3 Join the two areas by wiping the wet paint from both sections together.

color washing

Continue to wipe off the paint and glaze mixture with a large brush.

combing

Apply the base coat carefully and evenly so it is not too thick. Pull a comb firmly down over the glaze mixture in straight lines.

dragging

Apply the paint and glaze mixture in vertical stripes along the section you are working. Pull the dragging brush down several times to make a broken striped brush mark.

1 Apply a layer of paint on the surface, either a strong or soft paint that will wear through when rubbed.

2 Apply a coat of soft paint and allow it to dry.

3 Rub clear wax into the paint and allow it to sink in for a few minutes—don't be concerned if the paint darkens, it will soon return to its original shade.

4 Rub away with sandpaper, very lightly at first, to get a light textural look by removing the paint in certain places.

distressing

Distressing paint is a way of giving flat paintwork a texture. It is best if you use a soft paint so that rubbing back is not difficult. The paint should also be able to absorb wax to create a soft and mellow finish, and to help with the rubbing back. The wax will also protect the finish and can be polished.

Distressing can be done on wood using just one color, so when you rub through, the wood can be seen from underneath. If the wood is not attractive, such as a yellowish pine, then two colors can be used, so when you rub through, the color of your choice will be revealed. The art of this finish is to get the colors to work well together. Usually a darker color is used as a base color.

5 Fold the paper in half to make deeper lines in the paint.

6 Apply another layer of wax and buff it until the wood has a mellow, soft shine.

découpage

It is crucial to choose papers that are not too thick or shiny, and to apply enough varnish so the end result is not a raised picture—a good, high-build varnish should give this result after about five layers. The base color should also relate to the cutout pictures, too.

Cut out all the pictures you think you might need before you start. Place the designs onto your project, moving them around until you are happy with the placement before you begin to stick the pictures down. If you are working on a wall, use a little low-tack masking tape to figure out where the pictures will be placed.

1 Cut broadly around the picture before cutting closely around the outline of it, making sure there is a soft edge rather then a jagged line. Cut out the background of the picture as much as possible.

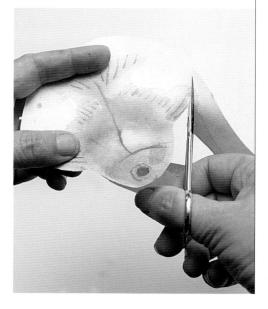

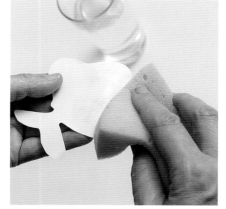

2 Dampen the picture lightly on both sides with water.

3 Coat an area of the base with découpage varnish, which also acts as the glue.

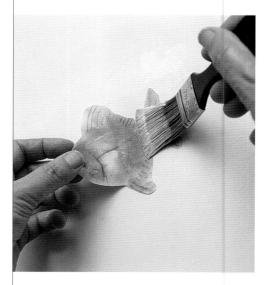

4 Place one end of the image on the glue before slowly pasting it down with the help of your brush, trying to remove any air bubbles.

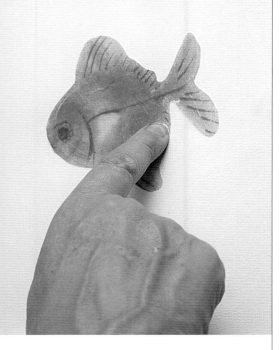

5 Press around the edges of the image to make certain they are completely glued down. Allow it to dry.

6 Varnish over the picture at least five times.

mosaic

A wide selection of tiles can be bought at craft stores and simply glued down with wood glue. Real mosaic uses tiles that are also grouted, but here we are using tiles that are simply glued. A mixture of tiles, buttons, plates, and stones can be used to make borders on windows and edges of furniture.

1 To get a clean break, nip the tile about halfway across with the end of the tile cutters.

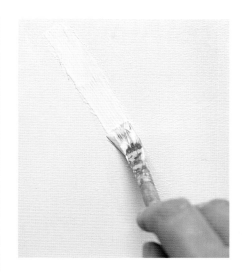

2 Apply glue either to the back of the tile or directly onto the base.

3 Put the mosaic in place and allow it to dry.

stenciling

The trick to good stenciling is to use very little paint. It can be applied with a small stencil brush or with a small sponge roller. The quickest way to do it is to use a roller and this also gives a charming, almost random look to the way the color falls. The finish is also flatter than with a traditional stencil brush.

2 Put the stencil in place, pressing down carefully, especially in areas with small, delicate tracery.

4 Alternatively, use a stencil brush. Place a very small amount of paint onto the end, getting rid of any excess paint by wiping it on some paper before starting. Wipe and stipple the paint over the stencil.

1 Spray the back of the stencil with repositioning glue and leave for a few seconds until the glue is ready to be used.

3 To get an even color across the design, use a roller that covers the entire stencil.

5 Blend two colors together, giving the design more density in some places than others.

printing

Printing can be done with anything that can be cut and can take paint. Potatoes have the distinct advantage of being easily obtainable. Sponges and polystyrene are also good materials to make prints with. None of these materials will make very accurate or detailed designs, unlike ready-made prints, but they do have a delightful way of giving a textured finish with each one being slightly different than the other. Be careful not to put too much paint on the printing block so that it squeezes out the side or results in a bumpy print.

1 Cut a potato in half with a very sharp and straight knife.

2 Draw an outline of the design roughly on the surface to help you cut it cleanly.

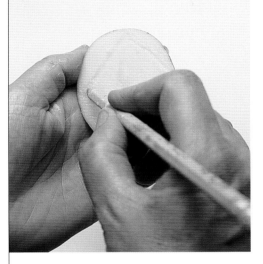

3 Cut out the design by slicing with a small, sharp knife.

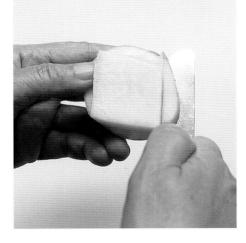

4 Wipe the potato before applying paint, as the surface will be very wet at first. Apply paint to the surface.

5 Press down on the surface with a lot of pressure, especially in the center of the potato, to make certain the print is reasonably solid.

the kitchens

the french country kitchen

Defined by its dusty, warm colors and use of eclectic, simple, but feminine furniture, French country style is growing in popularity. In this kitchen, an unconventional but elegant charm takes the emphasis away from the practicalities of modern cooking and cleaning units and moves toward creating a typically French retreat, peaceful and cozy for family entertaining.

This kitchen came together out of two decorating passions—collecting interesting things and using subtle whites. Although the palette of French country includes warm blues (see the colorboard on page 120 for inspiration) and muted greens and pinks, the dominant shades used here are whites and creams, which cannot be bettered for adding space and light.

Most of the eclectic finds come from searching through thrift shops; spotting new decoration is also part of the fun. If you gather exactly what appeals to you, you will soon have a collection, and then all you will need is some imagination to see how you can put things together. I have included suggestions here on how to use found objects and odds and ends to create new kitchen pieces. The advantages are that you will end up with unique pieces of decoration, not things from the same chain stores as everyone else. Of course, it does take time and patience—and is the opposite of instant decorating—but it will be personal to you and probably cheaper, which is always an added bonus.

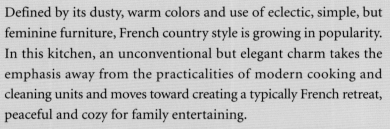

Right: Two narrow rooms have been integrated to make a kitchen/dining area, united by using lots of white, whimsical decoration, so the kitchen does not look too functional.

Above: A wooden "snake" over the door was a find from a country walk. Apart from being a delightful decoration it also serves to direct the eye outward, emphasizing the width of the room rather than the long galley shape.

inspirations

The look stems from the style of the château, a style that has its feet firmly in the eighteenth century. Châteaux are not necessarily very grand but elegance and a lack of clutter are hallmarks of the design style. The French look has a lightness of touch and is generally light in color, too.

Left: Painting the inside and outside of a cupboard with different colors is a charming French practice. The white edging on the shelves gives it a clean and tidy look.

Below: A farmhouse look can be achieved by painting woodwork. The large pine dresser and the table have been painted with duck egg blue paint, partly with a stain and partly distressed with a wax.

Above: The faded glory of an old mirror washed over with a gentle off-white matte paint, with traces of gold showing through, looks as though it has been freshly taken from the château.

Left: This elegant and uncluttered kitchen is reminiscent of a cool fresh dairy in an old French château. The milky whiteness and the rich yellowy creams of the paintwork, tiles, and china are offset by the coolness of the gray paintwork and the gray of the pewter plates.

Above: Simple wooden cupboards have been treated with white limed wax for the simple look of a French farmhouse.

french dresser

Who could imagine that this splendid dresser had been made from two pieces of rather plain furniture? It started life as a shelf unit and a small cupboard with drawers and has been given new legs, paints, and some decorative ornamentation. New knobs, a metal skirting trim, and decorative motifs have been added to make this an entirely original piece of furniture. Legs from an old chair have been cut, painted, glued, and finally nailed beneath the shelves to give them both height and elegance.

A matte chalk paint has been used, which has the advantage that you can easily remove sections of it with either water or wax to give a distressed finish. A few other neutrals are used, such as creams, grays, and beiges, with touches of blue and gold to keep it lively. A quirky touch was the painting of the sides and inner part of the dresser drawers in a dusty rose pink.

Always tackle any woodworking before painting and adding the decorations. This dresser went through many transformations as various ideas were tried out until the owner and maker were quite happy.

The dresser has an idiosyncratic charm, and its eclectic appeal gives the room a real sense of individuality. If a dresser is going to be decorated using items of one color, in this case white, each object must have an interesting shape of its own to give it a good profile against the cupboard. Here there is a good mixture of tall, round, and squat shapes in many different materials such as glass, china, silver, and brass. The scheme should not be too rigid, though, as the little red toy car at the base of the lamp testifies. Decorative items can be easy to find, but a collection might begin to look incongruous if it includes too much of a hodgepodge of ideas.

Collect things that you like: interesting hinges, knobs, and edgings, whether old or new, will all be useful in transforming furniture. Old chair legs, spindles, and broken frames can be found cheaply and plundered to use in your own furniture. Basic woodworking tools, such as a small hammer, screwdriver, saw, chisel, sandpaper, paint, and brushes, will all be needed.

Part of two old chair legs were sawn off to make stilts to raise the shelf, giving the dresser more height and character. A strip of brass edging found in a junk shop has been tacked onto the bottom shelf and, once painted, looks like a pretty lace trim.

Gray is the color of white in shadow, so painting the dresser back in this soft gray with a hint of blue (my Paris Gray chalk paint), gives the dresser depth, and helps outline the delightful decorative objects. Along the top of the dresser are three brass flower shapes, flattened brass candle holders, left over from a broken decoration. Tacked on to the corner and center, they are a humorous play on the more usual types of architectural ornament.

The inside and sides of one drawer have been painted a dusty pink and waxed, for special utensils, to match the drawer next to it, which has been lined with a beautiful handmade paper with pink dried flowers. In this drawer napkins and tablecloths are kept.

mosaic cupboard

Continuing the theme of white decorated with blue accessories, this unassuming wall cupboard unit, bought as standard, has been made into something a little different by adding some mosaic tiles, new knobs, and a lick of paint.

To match the dresser, the same gray and white paints have been used, with hints of gold paint. The cupboard has been transformed by decorating the edges of the glazed frames with mosaic tiles. Although the idea was to keep the look random and spontaneous, there is a certain structure. Themed in shades of blue, larger, darker-colored tiles are used at top and bottom to unify the piece, with lighter, smaller, glassy tiles used to bring glitter to the center; cobalt blue tiles frame the outside while paler turquoise tiles line the inside.

MATERIALS

All the tiles are left over from other jobs and the only pieces of equipment you will need are tile cutters and glue. You can also use larger tiles, but make sure they fit the borders of your cupboard or closet and are themed in shades of one color for unity.

Above: Some new glass knobs with a blue spiral were added to make a kitchen cupboard that does not look like any ordinary cupboard.

découpaged chest

Découpage is a fancy way of describing cutting out a paper design and gluing it to furniture with a coat of varnish. Explained in this way, the technique sounds banal but it can be an extremely beautiful and creative medium. The trick to good découpage is to cut out the designs well, apply enough of a high-quality, high-build varnish so that the paper design is not raised above the painted layer and does not look stuck on, and also to devise interesting paintwork as a base. This way, the end result is not simply a piece of paper stuck on a base.

There are some very beautiful wrapping papers available that can be used for découpage. I particularly like the ranges where the designs have been painted in watercolor so the result is a hand-painted look. Any thin piece of paper can be used. You can take images from anywhere, including scans or photocopies and images from the Web (as long as they are not copyrighted).

MATERIALS

Wrapping paper

Sharp scissors

10 fl. oz. glue varnish

30 fl. oz. découpage varnish

1 Use very sharp scissors to cut around the design, moving the paper rather than the scissors to ensure a smooth edge.

2 Cut out all the designs you think you will need and arrange them where you want them.

3 Dampen one of the designs on both sides, but don't soak it. This is to help stop the paper from bubbling.

4 Apply a coat of glue varnish to the surface where one of the designs is to be placed.

5 Stick the design down, starting from one end and brushing down to the other to try and avoid bubbles.

6 Allow it to dry a little and then varnish with at least five coats of découpage varnish. This is a thick varnish that allows you to build up enough layers to hide the bulge of the paper.

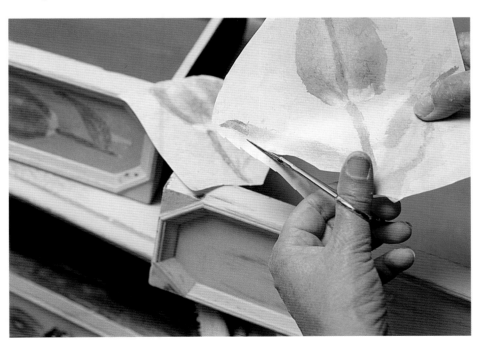

combed table

Gingham cloth is the very essence of French country taste and it is the inspiration for this tabletop that resembles a permanent tablecloth. This old table had beautiful legs but a replacement top made up of rough-and-ready planks, so I needed a design that would take the eye away from the shape.

The checkered effect was achieved by using a rubber comb, originally used for woodgraining, to make stripes, first in one direction and then the opposite. Although the comb does not make completely clean lines, especially when pulled over a rough base, the ragged effect makes the result look soft and yielding, like fabric.

Rubber combs are now often used to make decorative stripes. It is necessary to add glaze to the paint so that it remains wet enough to work with, but there must not be too much, otherwise the paint will be too transparent. You could also make your own comb out of cardboard, although these soon become waterlogged and will only last for the length of one project.

It has taken just five steps with Annie Sloan paint to transform this very basic tabletop into something very decorative for a cottage kitchen. As the idea was inspired by gingham, other base colors could be used, such as a tomato red for the base with the same old white for the glaze coat.

1 Rub down the top of the table with sandpaper to remove any old varnish or wax. Paint it a deep blue—Riviera Blue midsheen paint was used here—and allow to dry overnight.

2 Mix glaze into Old White chalk paint until the mixture becomes almost opaque.

3 Apply the white glaze in stripes—it was easy on this table because the top is made from planks.

4 Take a rubber comb with graduated teeth and pull down in a straight line. Repeat this on the entire tabletop. Allow the glaze to dry completely overnight.

5 Apply the same colored glaze the next day. This time comb at right angles. For protection, coat the table when dry in several coats of strong, water-based varnish.

MATERIALS

Sandpaper

30 fl. oz. Riviera Blue midsheen paint

20 fl. oz. Old White chalk paint

20 fl. oz. glaze

2-in. paintbrush

Graduated comb

40 fl. oz. water-based varnish

MATERIALS

Clear wax
4 oz. white pigment
1 oz. green or blue pigment
Fine wire wool
Cotton cloth

1 Mix some white pigment with a clear wax, combining it well to remove any of the clumps that occur naturally in the pigment. Before adding a colored pigment, ensure that the white is mixed well, so you can easily gauge the final color.

limed wood cupboards

The notion of limed wood comes from the nineteenth-century farmhouses whose paint was usually a whitewash made from lime. Reapplied each year, both as an antiseptic and a refresher for walls, when used on wood it was diluted and painted thinly, giving the typical bleached look. Limed wood is also sometimes called bleached wood because it is pale, as if it has been gently washed over with white.

It can be achieved in many ways, but one of the simplest is to use white wax. It can be bought ready mixed but it is easy to make and therefore simple to adjust to the exact color you want. Mix white pigment with clear wax, adjusting the color by adding a little blue or green pigment to suit the wood you are applying it to. This can both prevent modern pine from turning yellow or orange after a few years, and soften the brightness of new wood, while allowing the grain to show through. This method can be used on previously waxed wood where the varnish has worn away, and on floors, as well as furniture. Waxing works great because it feeds the wood, giving it a soft look with a mellow finish. If your kitchen units become dirty or dull with use, they can simply be revived with some clear wax. It is best used on wood with an obvious grain such as oak, elm, or old pitch pine.

2 Apply the mixture to the wood with a cloth or a piece of fine wire wool, pushing the wax into the grain by rubbing both with and across the grain. Allow it to harden for approximately five to ten minutes.

3 Wipe off the excess white wax, again making certain that the wax has reached all the grain.

4 Take some clear wax and wipe lightly over the wood with a cloth so that it adheres to the grain. If it comes straight off, then allow the white wax more time to harden.

the color-washed kitchen

Left: The wall has been color washed and stippled with pink and orange glaze to work with the tiles.

Top right: The color beneath the skylights becomes a richer raspberry pink, matched with a green-and-blue trim.

Below right: The color around the window is a deeper pink than the other walls.

This entire kitchen is bathed in brilliant color, and this has been achieved mainly with paint that echoes the richness of fruit—ripe mangoes, oranges, and raspberries. This kitchen is a good example of how to use color to bring out architectural features in a room. Built as an extension of the original house, the room includes part of the old building that makes a pillar in the center, and I wanted to make the most of, not conceal, the interesting mix of features. On the walls, irregularities of texture are enhanced by painting different shades of one color on opposing walls to make use of the various facets and levels of light throughout the kitchen.

The paintwork on the walls is not a straightforward flat color, but is applied more subtly, giving new depth and texture to the whole room. The rich and dense colors are achieved by using a color washing technique that mixes large quantities of paint with a little glaze.

The paint has been brushed and stippled, then worked to make cloudlike shapes with several undulating colors. The paintwork merges subtly and imperceptibly from orange to pink, and then on to deep raspberry. Looking at each wall, you are never sure if it is the color or the light that has changed.

For maximum brightness, the glaze can be made using pigments. Unlike paints, which are made with a mixture of colors (and may even include white or black pigment), glazes are very bright and clean, so it is easy to achieve very strong tones with them. For best results, paint over a base of bright white or yellow to give the final colors maximum impact.

inspirations

Glazing is one of the most versatile mediums in decoration, with many different finishes. As a medium, it crosses all style boundaries, being equally at home in both modern and traditional interiors. The most well-known use is color washing, but glaze is also used in combing, dragging, marbling, and frottage. Glaze can give your paintwork great depth, allowing you to put one color over another so both are visible, and also allows you to add texture.

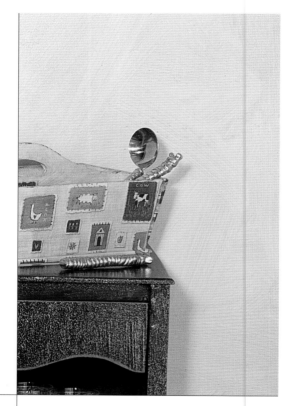

Right: Color washing in pale ocher yellows over cream is a natural way to give a wall color and texture. Here a large brush dipped into colored glaze was used.

Left: Glaze is a very good way to use bright, strong colors without them looking too overpowering and dense. Here, two layers of color have been applied, resulting in an energetic shade.

Right: A gray glaze has been applied over a plum-colored base in a modern interpretation of marble, using a roller and drops of water.

Left: Dragging is a very old technique, but here it is used with brilliant green and a daffodil yellow to create a very fresh effect.

Below: Adding glaze to paint loosens the mixture, allowing this simple checkered look to be created by combing the wet paint in long stripes across the tabletop.

frottaged wall

Frottage is a great technique for getting a bold but random effect on a wall. A sheet of crumpled newspaper is used to absorb the wet glaze, resulting in haphazard marks that sometimes expose large sections of the base color, while in other places making a delicate trace of lines where the crumpled newspaper has been.

Alternatively, you can use plastic drop cloths cut into strips so a whole length of a wall can be done at one time. These are applied by hanging them from the top of the wall and letting them drop down onto the wet glaze that has previously been applied in stripes rather than blocks. I worked with newspaper and painted with glaze to make the texture on this wall. Plain, flat gray was not strong enough to complement the other items in the room, so I decided to make a texture without much color. The trick is to be well prepared in advance. Have a good pile of paper or plastic sheeting cut and ready before you start.

A fairly deep bluish gray, Mud Gray was used as a base for the glaze mixture of Château Gray, bringing out the color's green tinges. The shades are very close to each other in tone— so much that the two colors merge into one if you close your eyes halfway—but they are significantly different in color. This makes a complex, yet neutral and interesting background for the brightly stained chairs.

MATERIALS

30 fl. oz. Mud Gray base paint

Old newspapers or plastic drop cloths

30 fl. oz. Château Gray glaze

1-in. paintbrush for glaze

1 Paint the wall and allow it to dry thoroughly. Crumple enough newspaper for the entire job.

2 Mix the glaze and apply it either to an area slightly larger than the newspaper, or in a stripe slightly wider than the plastic sheeting. Always leave a wet edge around the area on which you are working.

3 Spread the paper over the glazed section of the wall and run your hands firmly and evenly over the paper. Be careful not to take too long, because after a while newspaper will stick to the wall. Also be careful not to press your entire palm too firmly on the paper, as you may end up with a palm print through the paper.

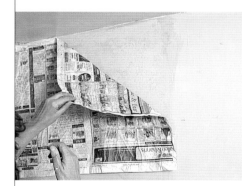

4 Remove the newspaper and discard it. There should still be a border of unfrottaged glaze, so you can work on the next section of glaze without any overlap that would make a darker line. Continue up and down the wall.

color washing & toning

When color washing, the paint is brushed and stippled to make cloudlike shapes and a subtle undulating color. Here, the paintwork merges subtly with the main color, and changes down the central column from lime green to emerald. Looking at the column, you are not sure if the color has changed or if it is the lighting.

For maximum brightness the glaze can be made using pigments. Unlike paints that are made with a mixture of colors and may include white or even black, pigment is very bright and clean so it is easy to achieve very bright colors. It is best to paint over a base color of white to give the color maximum impact.

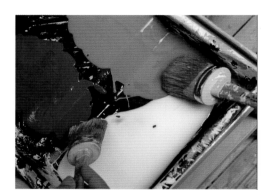

1 Take at least two paint colors and some scumble glaze. For this color wash the color is dense and not very translucent. To achieve this same look you must use a higher proportion of paint to glaze.

2 Use two big round brushes. This will help the paint manipulate easily, stippled and wiped. Use one for each color. The idea is to have two colors that blur imperceptibly. Start with one color and apply it in a balanced but uneven pattern on the area. You should be able to work an area of about half a yard square comfortably at a time.

3 Dip into the second color. Apply this color in the areas you haven't painted before and to some of the areas you have already painted.

MATERIALS

1-in. paintbrush
2-in. paintbrush
Two containers for paint
30 fl. oz. green chalk paint
15 fl. oz. dark blue chalk paint
15 fl. oz. Old White chalk paint
10 fl. oz. scumble glaze

Right: This wall has been color washed in a yellowy-green to match the tiles but contrast with the blue accent color wash.

4 Be careful not to cover the first color entirely, otherwise you will end up with one color rather than a subtle blend of colors. Also make sure not to leave too much of a distinction between the colors so you end with an obvious piebald effect.

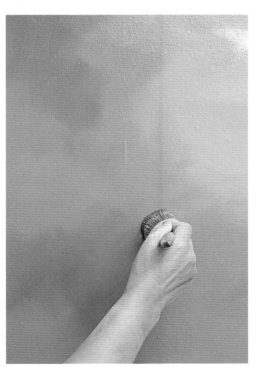

Soldier Red

A main color of a wash of Emperor's Red with Celadon Green and khaki-colored Château Gray.

Summer Flowers

Hawaiian Pink with touches of pastel blue Urban Light and Pink Silk.

reds
cherry, tomato, and apple

Chinese Chic

A strong impact made with Japan Red with Pale Yellow for contrast, and the deeper Sienna Yellow.

Red gives a room energy and lift. Using my colors, you can see the variety of effects red can achieve here. A little red goes a long way; one wall or a cupboard or just the insides of the cupboard and drawer linings would be ideal.

Red is generally quite a dark color, so use it only where there is a lot of light, especially if you are using a cherry red. If you want to use it where there is little light, then use a red with more of an orange hue in it, such as a tomato or strawberry red.

Like popping a tomato into a salad, reds look great with greens, especially soft sage and olive greens. And like strawberries, it works with cream!

Modern

A dulled red—made by mixing Emperor's Silk and Burgundian Reds—used with a dash of Silver Foil and Lilac Slate.

Chelsea Classic

The deep richness of the classic Burgundian Red mixes with the taupe warmth of Mud Gray and Creamy Linen.

Tutti-Frutti

The bright, cherry red of Hawaiian Pink with Celadon Green and Old White gives a lively Italian ice-cream look.

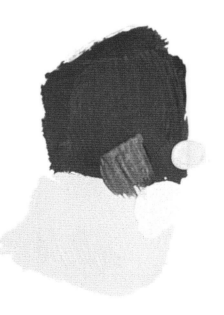

Napoleonic Classical

The classical Burgundian Red of Napoleonic France works well with Napoleonic Blue, Linen, and the warmth of Wet Clay.

City Slicker

Burgundian Red is a foil for Dry Cement and Urban Light with a dash of bright Japan Red.

the dragged kitchen

Dragging is an old technique used during the Georgian times. It originates from the practice of woodgraining, which was a method of painting in order to imitate wood realistically. A special, coarse-haired dragging brush, which is good for making the striated paint marks resemble grains of wood, is used. Dragging is done in two tones of brown and the effect of wood is very apparent.

Dragging has been used in this kitchen, but it is definitely not reminiscent of wood. The majority of the cupboards are dragged using soft ocher yellow glaze over a cream base, creating an easy and soft color. To give the room a little punch and vitality, the large larder cupboard is painted with a rich blue base with a dark, almost black, glaze lightly dragged over it so a lot of the blue is still apparent.

Both the walls and cupboards in this kitchen follow the usual approach of using a lighter color for the base when dragging. Sometimes a darker base coat is used with a lighter glaze over the top, but although this can give a very rich effect, it can look a little ghostly, especially if there is a lot of white in the glaze. The most important thing is to use a base coat similar in tone to the glaze—although a green glaze over a blue might be used if the two colors are fairly close in tone. Too much contrast can make the effect blatant and crude. Similarly, outrageous colors can be used as long as they are not screaming contrasts.

The large blue larder cupboard and the bookshelf at the far end of the room have been painted in a warm, rich blue with a near black glaze dragged effect. This gives an anchoring effect in the room and a sense of richness in a kitchen otherwise dominated by light, bright colors.

inspirations

This is a stylishly simple kitchen with a bright, contemporary feel. The dominant color is green, used both as a color in the cupboards as well as underneath the white and then allowed to show in certain areas.

Left: Yellow ocher and raw sienna yellows are earth tones and have a soothing effect, perfect for a busy family kitchen. Matched with the bright lettuce green of the walls, the kitchen has a clean freshness to it.

Below: The black stove punches a large hole in the wall, so it needs a strong color like this fresh, bright green to contrast it. The color also has softness, since it is textured like clouds.

Above right: The simplicity of the units contrasts with the brightness of the wall color, ensuring that the kitchen's character is not overcomplicated.

Above: Always drag in the direction of the grain of the wood so a panel will have vertical dragging.

Right: To achieve the rich colors on this dragged cupboard, the base color was an intense blue. A dragged near-black glaze tones down the color but lets the blue remain strong.

mutton cloth cloudy walls

1 Mix 30 fl. oz. of glaze and fold the mutton cloth into a round pad. Apply to the wall in a section the size of a small newspaper using a large brush. Make sure that the wall color can be seen through the glaze coat.

These walls have a delightful cloudy look—a bright, fresh green, like lettuce and green leaves, that looks sharp and smart and makes a great accompaniment to the deep, warm blue of the stove and the yellow ocher of the cupboards. The look has been achieved using a green glaze applied to a plain wall that is then partly removed by being gently dabbed with a pad of woven cloth while it is still wet. The cloth I used is called mutton cloth, but cheesecloth is very similar, and even some dishcloths can be used. The cloth must be soft with a coarse, open weave that gives a softly textured effect. It should be made from cotton, as this absorbs the paint more readily.

By dabbing more firmly in some places than others, a cloudy look is achieved. In some places it may be necessary to apply more of the glaze if you remove too much.

Use the same technique in different colors to make a sky—best painted on a white background using a blue glaze.

MATERIALS

30 fl. oz. green glaze
Mutton cloth or cheesecloth
1-in. paintbrush

2 Dab the wall to remove some of the paint and glaze mixture, but leave an area around the edge so the next section of glaze can be applied without creating a darker area where the two sections join. This is called keeping a "wet edge."

3 Dab the cloth more firmly over some parts of the wall, removing more of the glaze to reveal the base color beneath. In other areas, retain a little more of the color to create an uneven look. Apply the next section of glaze mixture along the previously applied wet edge. Work down and across the wall in blocks until finished.

With a dark stove, the color in this kitchen needs to be strong. This has been successfully achieved using a green with the contradictory properties of being fresh and zingy, as well as having a restful cloudy quality.

dragged cupboard

MATERIALS

20 oz. scumble glaze
10 fl. oz. blue paint
2-in. dragging brush
1-in. paintbrush

In this kitchen, dragging has been used twice in different colors. The main cupboards are done using soft ocher yellow glaze on a cream base, and on the big cupboard a rich blue has a dark, almost black glaze. The overall effect is fresh, rich, electric, and clean-looking. This technique is derived from wood graining and uses the brushes of that technique.

1 Paint the cupboard with the base color and allow it to dry. Now apply the glaze, making sure not to create a big buildup in the corners and tops. Remember, a little glaze goes a long way. Usually the glaze color is darker than the base color, but it can be the other way around. On the doors apply the glaze to the panel first, then work on the stiles and rails. The usual rule is to work from the large to the detailed areas. Apply the glaze in the direction of the wood.

2 Using a dragging brush or a coarse-bristled brush, pull the glaze down or across so you leave a broken striped effect. It is necessary to repeat the effect several times with the brush to take off enough of the glaze. You may need to wipe the brush with a cloth to take off any excess glaze, otherwise you will be putting glaze back on the surface.

3 Mottle with a cloth. Allow it to dry overnight, and for a richer look apply a second coat of colored glaze.

greens
lettuce, lime, mint, sage, olive, and white grapes

Green is a soothing, restful, and relaxing color for the kitchen. It is the most neutral of all the colors, being neither hot nor cold, and it is for this reason that green always needs another color to balance it. On the spectrum, green sits between the primaries yellow and blue. The range of greens is huge, spreading from sharp citrus limes to forest greens to all the bluish sea greens and turquoise.

Garden Fresh
Soothing Bamboo Green with a touch of fresh Antibes Green is perfect for a kitchen with a lot of whites.

South of France
Antibes Green shows the brightness of paintwork and foliage when mixed with Cream and Old Ocher.

Old Pottery
Jadelike Celadon Green, with green-tinged Château Gray and Old Ocher is reminiscent of traditional pottery.

1960s
Riviera Blue with Antibes Green and Old White has a retro 1960s look about it.

Cool

Louis Blue is a soft, pale, Madonna blue—making it the perfect cool antidote to the richness of Cairo Green.

Utility

Use olive Château Gray with the complementary Scandinavian Pink and a little Lilac Slate for warmth.

Cherry Orchard

Pastel Silk Pink, like Cherry Blossom, combines well with Leafy Bamboo and Celadon Greens.

Tudor

Amsterdam Green is a very deep green, and it needs the brightness of Ginger, lightened with a little white.

At the yellow end of the spectrum, the lettuce and lime greens have real pep. When these are muted they are warm and quiet, including gray-greens such as olive and sage green. These softer greens are the natural color choice for kitchens, matching the color of so many foods and offering more warmth than both the grass greens and aqua shades.

the modern kitchen

This is a large, light-filled, modern kitchen with lots of space. Although there is little obvious color apart from the wood, the steel, glass, and the white paintwork, the neutral palette does allow splashes of brightness and individuality. The original intention was to keep the colors very minimal. But after a while the owners felt the need for vibrancy, and for something a little less orderly than the rest of the room's strict architectural lines. For more restrained inspiration, you can also create the mural in neutral tones.

Left: Color inspiration for the horizontal stripes at the other end of the room was taken from the paintings of mugs on the wall above the dining table.

Left: The stunning impact of this room is made by the light bouncing off stainless steel, glass, and the shiny wooden floor. This is one large living space, with the kitchen at one end on a slightly raised floor, and a glass-tiled wall to separate it from the living room. In the kitchen, food preparation is focused on one side, with the dining table on the other. The painted wall provides a little restrained color to cheer up the dull days.

Above: The bright, shiny blue work surface is matched with the blue of the built-in fridge cupboard. The warm brown wood of the cupboards provides a soft neutral contrast to the blue.

inspirations

The modern kitchen tends to be large, often with a dining area, and takes inspiration from the concept of the farmhouse kitchen, where many activities took place along with cooking. Combining freestanding and built-in furniture helps to integrate a dining area, giving the feel of a family room. As a consequence, more color and interesting effects can be used.

Below: A great way to hide all the mess in the kitchen is to have really big cupboards and paint them.

Right: The basic Shaker-style wooden units have been merged with the modern materials of the stove and pans to create a solid base on which any sort of crazy color or object, such as the bright pink wreath of flowers, can be successfully added.

Above: The bright, melon pink against the brown of the cupboard is a wonderful and unusual combination of colors. Although both are strong, they are lightened by the stainless steel on the wall unit.

Left: Steel and industrial-influenced lighting create a modern take on the urban kitchen. The blue-gray of the woodwork echoes the steel, while the touches of wood soften the room.

modern mural

Add life and texture to a clean modern kitchen with this abstract mural. Horizontal stripes of various widths and color were painted on the wall using a sponge roller.

The lines are deliberately uneven to give it a freehand look. To keep the edges of the colors soft only one roller was used, and this was washed out between each paint application. But, of course, because the roller was a little damp, and the previous paint was a little moist, too, the line where the paints meet is not too hard, as it blurs slightly and bends.

First I planned my colors, choosing a larger group than I thought I would use. Six were chosen and, although I wasn't at first sure if I would use every single one, I kept my selection at hand while I was painting in case I needed them all. You won't need a lot of paint, so tester pots or colors left over from other jobs might be appropriate. Further tones can be made by mixing two of the colors. A dark and a light blue were the core colors, with some neutrals, too. The paint used has a slight sheen, as this works well in a room that contains several fairly shiny modern surfaces.

1 Pick some colors before you start. Very little paint is needed for a small area—about 3 feet wide by 5 feet high. I poured the colors into two roller trays with two sponge rollers.

2 Tape the edges of the wall using masking tape, which you will find is easy to remove.

3 I worked systematically by applying the first color on the top. Don't make the highest stripe too dark unless you want to lower the ceiling height. I chose fairly neutral colors from a similar tonal range but added a little dark blue in the center.

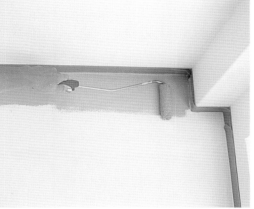

4 Between each color, wash the roller out thoroughly and squeeze out as much water as you can. Apply the second color, making a thinner or thicker line.

MATERIALS

one 2-in. sponge roller
one 4-in. sponge roller
masking tape
soft cloth or rag
two roller trays for paint
10 fl. oz. off-white chalk paint
10 fl. oz. cream chalk paint
10 fl. oz. mid-gray chalk paint
10 fl. oz. dark gray chalk paint
10 fl. oz. light blue chalk paint
10 fl. oz. dark blue chalk paint

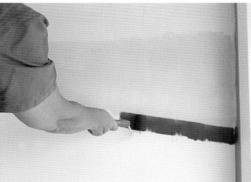

5 Continue rolling stripes of varying colors and widths. Don't worry too much if the colors go wrong, as you can always go over a color with a fresh coat when the first has dried.

spotty marble table

1 Prepare the surface of your table and cover it with a midsheen purple paint. Make a mixture of two parts glaze to one part cream paint. When applied, the mixture should not be so thick that it comes out opaque. The purple base color should always be visible through the glaze mixture.

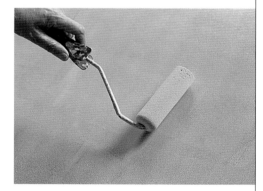

2 Apply the glaze evenly across the table with a sponge roller. If you are getting lines from the edge of the roller, just run the roller very gently over the marks to obliterate them.

Marble is a common surface in a kitchen, and there are many ways to imitate its appearance with paint. The method used here is a development of just one of the techniques employed in painting an accurate rendition of marble. This effect can only be achieved when painting on a horizontal surface, so you could also try this on a floor.

On this old dining room table, a modern interpretation has been given to painted marble. Although any base color can be used, a fairly dark color seems to work best, as it helps to give a sense of depth and solidness.

This kitchen, as a whole, combines a complex mix of bright, more or less primary colors used next to a series of neutral tones. The six kitchen chairs around the table were clear and bright, so a strong neutral tone was needed for the table.

To match the rest of the room, the table has been painted Plum and then the top is covered with a mixture of cream and gray, so the finished color is taupe.

You have to work fairly swiftly to achieve this technique, so turn off the phone and work without interruption. Once armed with all your materials it is very quick, so go for it!

MATERIALS

20 fl. oz. Plum midsheen paint
2 sponge rollers
40 fl. oz. scumble glaze
10 fl. oz. cream paint to color glaze
10 fl. oz. second color for glaze
Two 1-in. paintbrushes
50 fl. oz. clear wood varnish

3 While the glaze is still wet, drop water onto the surface in small spots. It can be difficult to see it but if you look at it from an angle you should be able to see where the water has fallen. Allow the water to sit for a few minutes.

The plum and gray paints of the table make a colorful, neutral taupe color that contrasts well with the brighter, primary colored chairs.

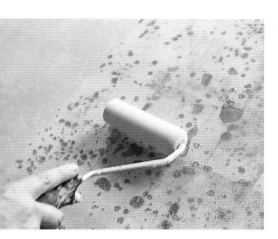

4 Take a dry sponge roller and roll it gently over the tabletop. The spots of water will be drawn up into the sponge, making areas of purple clearer.

5 When the surface is dry, a second layer of color can be spread over the table. Finally, varnish it entirely two or three times for protection and depth.

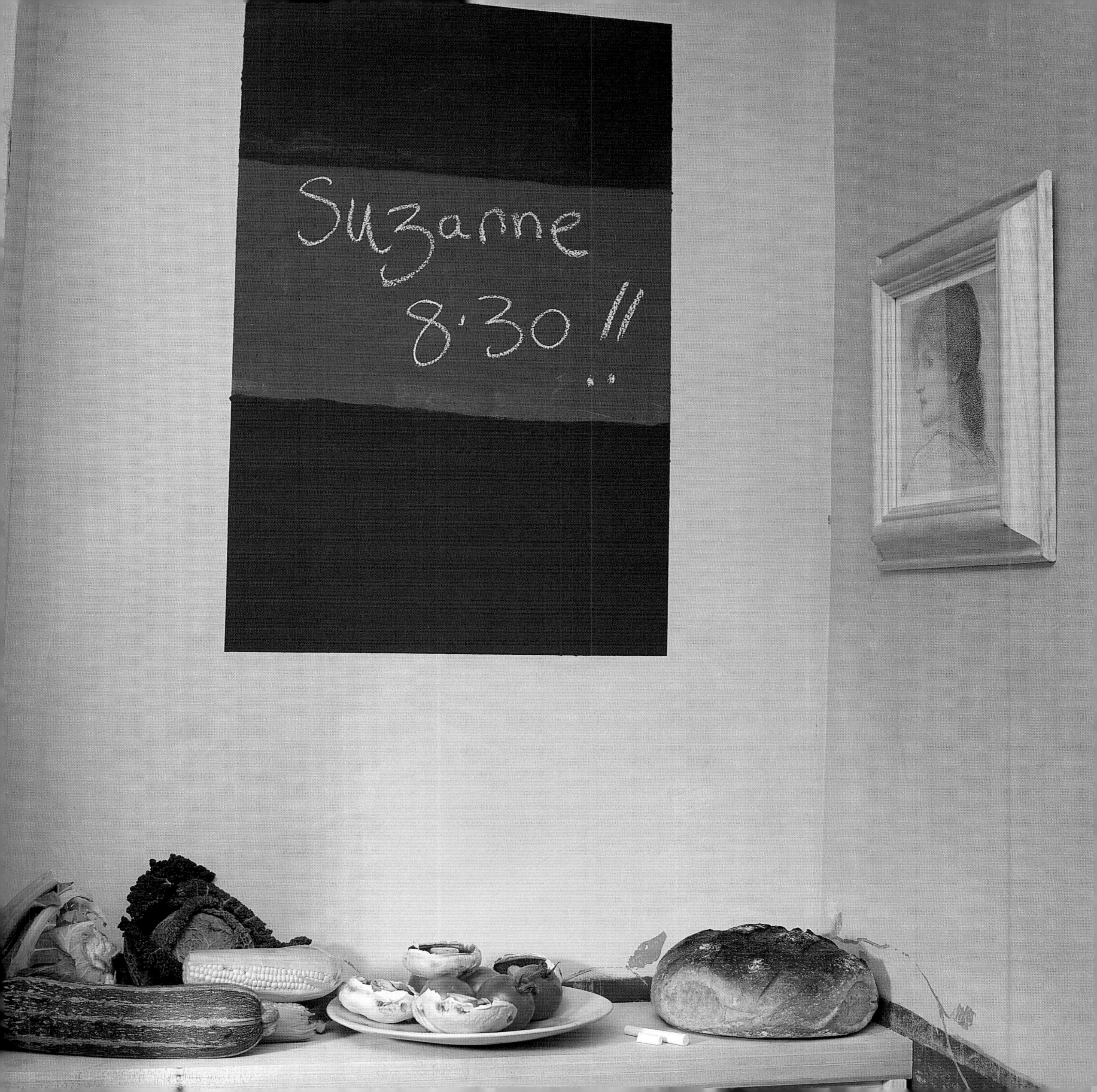
Suzanne
8.30 !!

blackboard

A large blackboard in your kitchen will change your life! It is a great place to write notes and reminders. Using the chalk paint, you do not have to confine yourself to the traditional black paint, but take any color that is dark enough to allow white chalk to show up.

MATERIALS

20 fl. oz dark chalk paint
Roll of masking tape
1-in. paintbrush

1 Mark an area of the right size with paper masking tape on the wall.

2 Paint the area inside the tape with a color or stripes of color of your choice. Give it a second coat so there is a good solid layer.

3 Remove the masking tape and leave it to dry thoroughly overnight.

4 Once you have written on it, you can wipe it clean with a damp cloth. You may notice that this causes a little bit of the paint to be removed, but this will only happen the first few times.

varnished dresser

When wood has a really attractive grain, it is a shame to hide it by painting over it. Varnishing may be the best solution, but if the color of the wood is a hearty brown, at best, or a sickly orange, at worst, the answer is to mix some pigment with the varnish so that the color is softened but the grain of the wood is still visible. By mixing your own varnish mixture, it is possible to vary the opacity and strength of color in the varnish.

Use a clear, water-based varnish—oil varnishes yellow with time—in either matte or the more robust satin finish. If you do want a matte finish, then mix satin varnish with white pigment for the base, and cover with a straight matte coat.

White is not the only other color that could be used; choose from the thousands of pigments available. Any could be used to give your white a hint of color, or used on their own. If you find pigments hard to obtain, then you can use colorizers that are liquid tints, although this will not give you as much control on the final color of the varnish.

MATERIALS

Sandpaper

4 oz. white pigment

20 fl. oz water-based matte or satin varnish

1-in. varnish brush

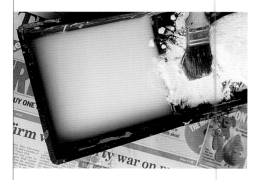

This smart cupboard has been decorated with a white varnish to help bring out the subtle pinkish color from underneath. With a light green painted interior the effect is delicate and pretty, helping to make a large piece of furniture seem light.

1 Rub down with sandpaper, if the wood is new, to make certain the finish is smooth. Prepare a container and pour out the varnish.

2 Add white pigment to the varnish and mix well. Before starting, make certain that no lumps remain in the pigment.

3 Apply smoothly with a soft brush, making sure to cover the wood consistently.

4 Keep a wet edge to each section to avoid overlaps drying into darker areas. Work systematically through defined sections—once you start on a panel, finish it before continuing.

Left: Lighthearted and undemanding, spots are a delightful and unpretentious way to decorate a kitchen. Because several colors can be used, it is a good way to introduce a variety of shades into the room.

MATERIALS

30 fl. oz. midsheen paint

Roller tray

1-in. paintbrush for each color

Total of 10 fl. oz. flat paint in three to four colors for the spots

Spotty roller

2-in. paintbrush or large roller

1 Paint the wall a color that is a mid to dark tone.

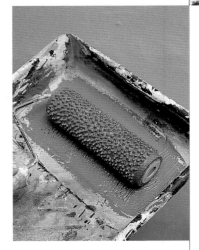

2 Pick a variety of paints—leftovers and tester pots might be enough for one wall. Pour a small amount of paint into a large roller tray; just the tip of the nodules should be covered with paint.

3 Alternatively, use a lightly loaded 1-in. brush to paint only the tips of the roller with a color.

spotty wall

Painting a kitchen wall with spots is an ideal way to give a room a lighthearted and fun feel. A rubber roller covered with small nodules makes spots when paint is applied and rolled across the wall in many directions. By using different colors you can make it as colorful as you like. Choose a theme—mine was a garden—as it helps to focus the number of colors you apply. If you are not too careful, the whole thing can get gaudy and discordant with too many colors applied. Three or four is probably the maximum you need.

Another theme might be a night sky with twinkling stars in pastel colors. Instead of a flat background, you could color wash the wall to create a more uneven and interesting base for the spots.

This technique looks best when it is applied to a deep or medium-toned color rather than a pale one, as it gives the spots depth and solidity. Choose a main color for the spots with a second, third, or fourth color for the highlights. A small amount of a lighter color is a good idea. Also, remember to work the roller in different directions, not just up and down; where spots overlap curious patterns emerge.

4 Roll the implement on the wall in different directions. When you get to the ceiling and other edges of the wall that the roller cannot cover, fill in the spots by hand if the area is not too large.

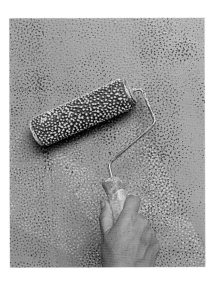

neutrals
milk, nuts, and oatmeal

Stone Beach
Biscuit-brown Wet Clay evokes a feeling of comfort when combined with Bleached Canvas and Mud Gray.

Blanket Box
Mud Gray is the main color, with the blue tinge of Dry Cement and Linen.

Mossy Bank
Château Gray with Linen and Dry Cement.

Scandinavian
Duck Egg Blue mixes shades of blue and green. It can be distressed when used with Paris Gray and Old White.

Chic

Sophisticated Paris Gray is detailed with a little Ginger and Chateau Gray to perk it up.

Architectural

The warm woody tone of Wet Clay is the perfect foil for Dry Cement and Linen.

Parchment

Mud Gray is a beautiful and complex color that softens when used with Old Ocher and Linen.

Nordic Sky

The bluish gray of Dry Cement has great depth in contrast to the Old Ocher and Old Violet.

One of the features of modern kitchens is the use of contemporary materials such as stainless steel or glass. The focus is on the materials rather than the color of the walls or decorations. So many contemporary kitchens use very little color, so there is no color conflict with the materials.

White is probably the most often used color in the kitchen, partly because it is clean and fresh looking. It can look clinical or have the traditional look of the dairy with the off-white colors of milk and yogurt.

There are a myriad of grays and beiges, all with their own distinctive character. There are also grayed greens and blues, which are a way of adding a little gentle, neutral color.

the distressed kitchen

This contemporary kitchen makes its mark with a brilliant splash of clear blue. The maximum impact is made here by using colored glass as a backsplash. This particularly strong turquoise blue was only developed in the twentieth century, and its modern feel makes it an ideal accompaniment to the stainless steel in the room.

The vibrant color and shiny texture dominates the room. Used in combination with softer textures, both the painted wooden units and the wooden work surface are coated with a glossy satin finish, as well as a more delicate texture. The white units share a two-tone paint effect, combining the original blue and the deeper blue that is also used for the cupboard interior. The wooden units were first painted with Riviera blue and Pacific blue, which were dabbed onto the surface to create a mottled effect. A coat of Old White chalk paint was brushed over the whole surface and allowed to dry. While still freshly done, but dry and easy to remove, the chalk paint was wiped lightly with water so the blue could surface from beneath. Finally it was varnished for a long-lasting effect.

inspirations

In an age of slick, mass-produced decorations and furniture with featureless, sprayed-on varnish, we long for individual pieces suggesting character and individuality. The distressed look can resolve this. It suggests activity and family life, where children's pictures, postcards from friends, and the general day-to-day knickknacks sit alongside kitchen paraphernalia.

Whether the distressed approach to decoration in the kitchen is inspired by the farmhouse look, the French château, or a more modern look, it is an easy style to live with.

Right: The battered, old green chair by the warm stove is well worn but much loved. If you have a large enough kitchen, the distressed farmhouse style can work well.

Below: The distressed method does not have to evoke nostalgia, but instead can be a way of picking up on color. The warm natural pink, very popular in Scandinavian painted furniture, on the inside of the cupboard can also be seen in touches on the front.

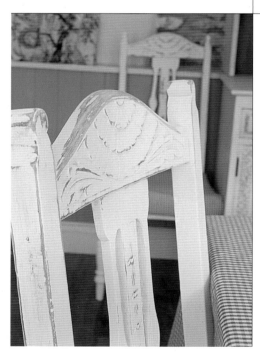

Above left: In the modern kitchen that incorporates a lot of stainless steel, distressing can create a more delicate mood. The paint has been washed off the cupboard gently with water so that touches of another color are revealed.

Left: These chairs have been given the scrubbed and trim look of the French style by being painted a clear white rubbed back with wax.

distressed waxed cupboard

Inspired by earth tones, this welcoming kitchen is reminiscent of the colors of summer, updated for a peaceful contemporary look. Drawn from nature, the paints—red oxide, yellow ocher, and sage green—are based on age-old pigments extracted for centuries from the countryside. The lines of the cupboard are simple and clean, while the decoration enhances the clean look and introduces texture and gentle color. The finished effect is of cupboards that have a naturally textured look, and although the colors are gentle, a wide variety of shades appears the closer you move to appreciate them.

To create this effect, the first coat was a simple green and the second a mottled mixture of ocher, cream, and off-white. Using a simple technique, the paint is slowly striated with a piece of cardboard and textured to show a dusty sage beneath. As a final touch, the paint was waxed, then rubbed away with sandpaper and a soft cloth to reveal the green and, in some places, the wood underneath. Wax is a wonderful way to treat cupboards in a kitchen, as it absorbs into the chalk paint, making the units water-resistant so they can be wiped clean.

1 Seal the wood with one coat of wood sealer. Paint the cupboard surface all over with a deep gray-green chalk paint.

2 Apply a coat of chalk paint in a mixture of cream, Old White, and Old Ocher paint, mottling the strokes so the finished effect is not a flat color.

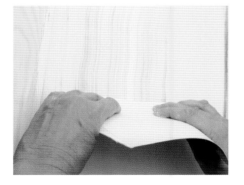

3 On the panel of the cupboard, while the second layer is still wet, pull a piece of torn cardboard downward over the surface to make a slightly striated effect. Allow to dry thoroughly.

4 Using a soft brush, apply wax in light strokes over the whole surface. Repeat the application if you want a particularly shiny and protected finish.

5 The final finish is achieved with wax applied and then sanded and rubbed through to create a distressed look. Use fine-grade sandpaper on patches of the cupboard and rub areas of paint gently until you have revealed the paintwork.

MATERIALS

Two 2-in. paintbrushes

Fine-grade sandpaper

Soft cloth or rag

Soft brush

Torn cardboard

Container for paint

Container for coating

25 fl. oz. wood sealer

30 fl. oz. Celadon Green chalk paint

15 fl. oz. cream chalk paint

15 fl. oz. Old White chalk paint

15 fl. oz. Old Ocher chalk paint

30 fl. oz. liquid paste wax

6 Using a soft cloth, buff up the entire surface of the cupboard. The more layers of wax you apply, and the more you buff, the higher the shine and the protection of your units will be.

french distressed chairs

MATERIALS

Sandpaper
8 oz. clear wax
30 fl. oz. Old White chalk paint
Two 2-in. paintbrushes
Cloth for application of wax
Polishing cloth

The shape and carving of these chairs made them potentially charming. But in their original state they looked drab and plain. I decided on a simple, one-color, distressed effect, comprising a single coat of paint over brown wood. The soft effect is created by covering the chair with wax before rubbing it away in places with sandpaper, taking the malleable chalk paint with it. A second and third layer of clear wax is then applied to make a beautiful and long-lasting finish. This gives them a simple, rustic appeal, as if they had been painted with limewash that had worn away over the years. It is up to you to decide how much paint you want to remove. The best places to remove paint are the backs and the feet—the areas that receive most handling.

Remember not to give your distressing an even feel—if you only use one pressure you will achieve a distressed look that is contrived and crude, rather than create an interesting patina. To give the chairs a prettier, less basic feel, paint them a pale color, perhaps blue, beneath the white before distressing.

1 Sand the chairs to remove any varnish, particularly over the areas where there is a lot of contact with hands, such as the backs and feet. This is particularly important for older furniture, since the varnish might be loose, or an old stain might leach through to the new paint layer.

2 Paint with Old White chalk paint, giving it two coats to cover it entirely—particularly over dark wood. Avoid missing sections by first turning the chairs upside down to paint the underside.

3 Apply a generous amount of clear wax with either a brush or a cloth. Work in the paint, concentrating on a small area, perhaps half of the back of the chair at a time.

4 Rub over the waxed and painted chairs with medium-grade sandpaper where you would like to remove the paint. Rubbing over any carved areas immediately gives definition, and rubbing hard in some places and lighter in others will vary the texture.

5 Apply more wax and polish. The more layers of wax applied, the higher the shine.

The carvings on the backs of the chairs have been emphasized by painting them white and distressing. With blue gingham seat covers and toile de Jouy curtain fabric, the kitchen has an effortless appeal.

The interior of the cupboard has been painted in the deeper of the two blues to make a delightful backdrop for glasses and the white and blue china. This contrasts with the distressed exterior, where in some places only the turquoise layer of chalk paint is revealed, and in others the deep blue shows through.

water-distressed cupboard

This kitchen combines shiny modern materials with the softness of traditional finishes, making it an approachable family kitchen—the key is to choose a modern color that sits happily with both wood and softly distressed white paint. The units were first painted with Riviera and Pacific midsheen blue paints before being covered with Old White chalk paint. The softer paint was then gently washed over with a damp sponge to reveal one or both of the blue layers underneath. Although this technique is called distressing, when used with modern colors the idea is not to age the units but to give them a softer, more colorful look.

1 Paint splashes of two shades of midsheen paint. Allow them to start merging, but stop before they lose their own identities.

2 Apply a thin top coat of a lighter-colored chalk paint evenly across the unit and allow to dry.

3 Take a damp cloth or sponge and wash some areas free of the white paint until the blues beneath are revealed. Wash over the entire area of white gently, concentrating on the areas around the handles and panel edges.

MATERIALS

10 fl.oz. Riviera Blue midsheen paint
10 fl.oz. Pacific Blue midsheen paint
20 fl.oz. Old White chalk paint
1-in. paintbrush
Cloth or sponge
20 fl. oz. water-based varnish
1-in. varnish brush

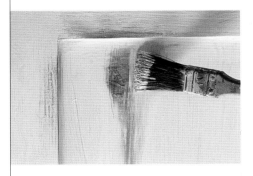

4 When dry, finish by applying strong, water-based varnish. Repeat if necessary when dry.

the pink kitchen

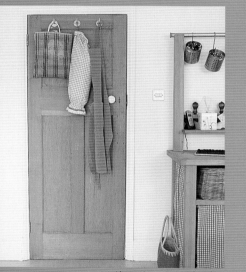

Above: Attention to detail in all matters pink! Keeping to a color theme helps to keep a room tidy even when there are lot of disparate objects, from shopping bags to the aprons hanging on the door.

This kitchen has a large, airy, and modern look about it and has been designed to develop with a growing family. The basic design is very simple, cool, and plain. The walls are white with gray in the stainless steel and blue-gray painted cupboards, with some pale wood, too. All this makes a neutral background for colorful objects and decoration. Using this formula, almost any color could be chosen as the accent color to complement the neutral base.

Reds and pinks have been growing in popularity for the kitchen. Imported for use in private homes from restaurants, pink is traditionally a dining color because it is said to promote relaxation. Here, a brilliant shocking pink has been chosen to transform a neutral kitchen. It is as if the color has been thrown at the room in great splotches to add as much energy and life as possible for a playful, modern feel.

Instantly noticeable, the pink accessories include baskets, glasses, lights, boxes, rugs, pictures, and even a pink computer. The great thing about incorporating color using accessories is that your transformation is ongoing: you can continue adding more pink items as and when you find them, and then incorporate pink using the painting projects on furniture and single walls, too. Importantly, this method of design also allows you to change the room after a few years, should you ever want to try a completely new color.

Right: A place where children can play and work while you cook is a great idea for modern-day living. Pink is the operative color and this workbench has been decorated in gingham, with pink boxes, bags, and lots of incidental decorations.

pink-stained cupboard

This new cupboard made from pine presented an ideal opportunity to create a stain. The idea of a stain is that the wood absorbs the color, emphasizing its natural tones. Paint, on the other hand, forms a solid layer over the top of the wood. Staining also allows the wood grain to show through.

The joy of creating a stain from paint, rather than buying a prepared one, is that I could choose the exact tone of pink—here I used my Scandinavian pink as a base, made from earth-red ocher, covered in white to create this very natural shade. Remember that if wood has been previously varnished or waxed, you will have to remove this before staining.

1 Cover the cupboard with a sealant to seal all the knots in the wood.

2 Mix 30 fl. oz. of Scandinavian pink paint with the same amount of water and stir together.

3 Apply the stain with a sponge, keeping a wet edge to ensure the joints do not dry to different shades.

4 When the entire dresser is covered, create an even finish by wiping off any excess stain with a water-soaked sponge.

5 To soften the stain, mix white paint with water and apply in the same way, again removing any excess stain with a sponge.

MATERIALS

30 fl. oz. dark pink paint

10 fl. oz. white paint

30 fl. oz. sealant

Two 1-in. paintbrushes

Mixing container

Sponge

Right: Over the years this cupboard will age beautifully as the pine becomes darker and turns a more orangy yellow. The earthy pink color of the cupboard will develop into the rich tones of a ripe melon.

The base of this wall is my Hawaiian Pink, a midsheen paint. Over this, a glaze of lighter cream was wiped and partly swirled. By using white in the glaze, the color is made a little more opaque. A second coat of glaze—this time of clear pink—was then wiped all over. Since the wall is in a kitchen it was varnished for durability. The chair in front is a new one that I painted with a mixture of green pigment and yogurt. This was then left unvarnished, and I have allowed it to age naturally for over three years.

translucent color-washed wall

This is a way of making a wall look as though it is filled with a subtle, yet bright and vivacious, color. Color washing is a way of giving a wall depth and liveliness.

Create the effect by mixing paint with scumble glaze, a transparent medium that keeps the paint from drying too quickly—allowing you to move the paint around on the wall to make marks in whatever way you want—and also gives the opaque paint a translucent quality.

On this wall I wanted great depth and solidness, so I have applied two layers of a vividly colored glaze.

MATERIALS

30 fl. oz. Hawaiian Pink paint

2-in. paintbrush

60 fl. oz. scumble glaze

30 fl. oz. paint for glaze

1-in. paintbrush for glaze

Cloth to remove paint and glaze mixture

1 Paint the wall in a solid layer of the base color and allow it to dry thoroughly.

2 Mix two parts glaze with one part paint and apply the mixture evenly across the wall.

3 Wipe off some of the glaze. It can be done in swirls or by wiping it in every direction, as if you are dusting the wall. If you are going to apply a second coat for depth, allow it to dry overnight.

4 Optional: Apply a second coat of glaze. You can mix this in a darker or lighter tone. If you have previously made swirls, it may be best to soften them now by wiping in different directions.

Heather

Amsterdam Green and Bamboo Green are balances for a mixture of Lilac Slate and Old Violet.

Nordic Blues

Deep and gray Old Violet is softened with Louis Blue, perhaps used over it and distressed.

pinks and purples
eggplant, plum, grape, and melon

1940s

Lilac Slate is a pretty, pale purple—restrained with the addition of Château Gray and Mud Gray.

Victorian Violets

A mixture of Old Violet and Lilac Slate is used with Old Ocher and Old Violet like a pretty posy.

Pink is a new color for the kitchen. There are two main groups of pinks and they have very different characteristics. The shocking pinks, like watermelon pink, are bright, luscious, and alive with a real strength about them. This works well with turquoise and aquamarine. When they have white in them, they become the soft pinks of strawberry and cherry yogurt.

Swedish Inspiration
Sienna Yellow with a wash of Old Ocher distressed over a base of Scandinavian Pink.

Tuscany
Use Old Ocher with earthy Primer Red and lots of pale, red oxide Scandinavian Pink.

Traditional pinks are the Tuscan pinks that have a hint of brown about them, suggesting reddish ocher as their base. These browner tones are also the pinks of salmon and shrimps, and work well with creamy yellow ochers and grayed blues and greens.

Famille Rose
To recall pretty Chinese porcelain, use a Burgundian wash on a white background, with Bamboo Green and Linen.

Mexico
A mixture of Spanish Orange and Old Ocher makes a spark with Hawaiian Pink and Spanish Orange.

Shockingly Pink
The pale, pastel Pink Silk and the bright Hawaiian Pink is softened by a little Primer red.

african fusion kitchen

Although the built-in cupboards are standard units, they stand out in ocher and spicy brown for an individual look. Tiles from Tunisia make a strong and colorful focal point behind the stove.

The colors, textures, and light of Africa are a rich source of inspiration. From the north, you can find delight in the fertile colors of Morocco and Tunisia, with tile work and the traditional smooth plaster finish of the walls. This is a verdant world with lots of verdigris greens and rich coppery oranges, alongside amethyst purples and sapphire blues with brassy gold.

From other parts of Africa comes the tradition of using a sparse palette to great effect, working with little more than stark black and white with flashes of yellow ocher and gold. Splashes of red and lush grass green have been added to this simple mix. From West Africa and the southern Sahara with its famous Tuaregs there is the long-established use of indigo blues. In East Africa the Arab influence is still apparent and from the Cape and South Africa you will see an effervescence and multicultural style of decoration.

Texture is important when using African colors; thick and impasto, washed and wiped, dense and opaque, shiny or matte, all add to the finished effect. Mixed with European traditional design, African paints and styles can be innovative and refreshing.

inspirations

The old, softly undulating plaster walls of this cottage are reminiscent of similar walls in Africa. They have been color washed in light and delicate warm yellow ocher by applying paint over the walls with a cloth, before wiping it to bring out all the nuances of texture. The panels (left and below) are a familiar shape in Europe, and although inspired by panels seen in an Italian palazzo, the colors and shapes also suggest Africa.

Above: The old cupboard, painted in a powerful teal blue with ginger on the molding, makes a great impact in a mainly yellow and red ocher kitchen. The blue echoes the similar color in the painting of the Masai people above.

Above: In contrast to the wash of the panels and wall, the white outline and the small, dark squares at the panel's corners are painted in opaque paint to give both definition and contrast.

Left: The wall cupboard is painted with two yellow and one dark red ocher. Hanging from the cupboard door is a string of seed pods, shells, and fragments of ostrich shells from Africa echoing the colors of the room.

polished plaster

This soft and glossy paint finish is inspired by African ideas from Morocco and Kenya. The silky smooth texture of the walls owes its finish to the *tadlakt* paintwork of Morocco, where a lime plaster is applied before being smoothed over and polished with a special stone until shiny smooth. Here I have reworked the idea in both white (left) and a fiery red-oxide orange (below), which is also a traditional mid-African color. You can try any bright color for this effect, but always use chalk paint.

The wall of niches is developed from the Arab-influenced interiors of Lamu Island in Kenya, where cliffside homes come accompanied by small niches, dug into rock walls, that provide a cool place for storage. Here, without a rock face to dig into, the idea had to be reinterpreted. The niches were built out from the brick wall and plastered to make little rounded arches. They were then painted and rubbed with fine sandpaper until perfectly smooth.

1 Apply the paint to a smooth wall. The smoother the base surface and application, the easier it is to achieve a smooth finish. If you prefer a more rustic look, then make brush marks and start by working on an uneven wall.

2 Take very fine-grade sandpaper and rub it over the surface well. Using water will make the process too wet and messy, so it is best to do this dry. For speed, you could use a sanding machine over a large surface. This may alter the color—making it slightly lighter—and may emphasize any indentations. But if lumps and bumps remain the area will have a more interesting finished texture.

3 Finally, buff with a cloth to remove dust and give a final polish.

yellows
lemons, corn, pineapple, oranges, and papaya

Oriental Zing

Pavilion Yellow with Old White and Ginger matches the silk robes of an emperor.

Madame Pompadour

The pale ocher of Limestone with a little Lilac Slate and Mud Gray.

Posy

The pale yellow primrose of Straw is balanced by Old Violet and Paris Gray.

New Deal

Combining yellow and gray was popular in the 1950s, re-created with Pale Yellow, Dry Cement, and Urban Light.

Sunny, bright, and optimistic, yellow is a great color for a kitchen that gets little light. At night, however, the yellowness of lights can obliterate the yellow in the room, leaving only the greens and grays. Overcome this by choosing tones toward the orange part of the spectrum.

Yellows range from sharp citrus lemon to the earthy ochers—the nearest we get to a dark yellow. Orange is an underused color that looks great with earthy pinks and creams, as well as dark orange, more commonly known as terra cotta. Bright yellow with the grays of stainless steel, granite, and slate brings a zing to a modern kitchen.

Florence

The sienna yellow of Moroccan Walls with Paris Gray and Old Ocher recalls old Italian buildings.

Venice

The ocher of Moroccan Walls combines well with Ginger, Chateau Gray, and Amsterdam Green.

Ice Cream

The vanilla yellow of Cream with the soft strawberry of Pink Silk makes a delicious ice-cream sundae.

Old Amsterdam

Pale and creamy Limestone with touches of the deeper Sienna Yellow and Cairo Green.

making pictures

Pattern making and stenciling are both very old ideas—some of the finest furniture has been stenciled, découpaged, and hand painted. It is also a way of making simple pieces of furniture look special and individual, and, of course, walls and entire rooms can be painted, too.

When using stencils and printing blocks, even those with less confidence in their artistic abilities can produce beautiful decoration. There are now hundreds of stencil designs from all periods and parts of the world available, from complex Oriental carpets to Art Deco "wallpaper." As real wallpaper is not a good idea in a kitchen, you could use stencils to create your own. Stenciling on walls normally involves the creation of simple borders, but now bolder figures, more subtle colors, and entire wall decorations are being used.

Printing is a particularly good way of making naive designs and simple geometrics. There are many fine design stamps of a sophisticated quality that can be bought, too.

If you are more confident, you could also incise patterns in paint directly onto surfaces by drawing directly into wet paint—a good technique for those people who can draw but don't feel confident to paint freehand. The panels on kitchen cupboards provide an ideal area to show off your individual talent by making your own framed pictures, whether you choose to use stencils, découpage, printing, or freehand painting. Maybe you should try each panel with a different design!

Right: This pretty blue, yellow, and white kitchen has a blue sponge-stamped border inspired by the jug on the draining board. The border goes around the room on the pelmet, giving the room a light and undemanding decorative edging.

Left: A border in blue, suggesting tiles or a mosaic, can be created with just a square sponge and some paint. The sponge will not give a perfect painted look all over, so the effect is hand painted and individual.

Far left: The milky white walls in this dairy-style kitchen have small, delicate stencils in gray, a cool way to add pattern without clutter.

inspirations

Making pictures and patterns is a great way to put your individual imprint on your kitchen. Because the kitchen is where you create your meals, it is the most creative part of the house—stenciling, stamping, and freehand painting are an extension of this. Even if you do not feel confident enough to paint your own pictures freehand, it is possible to achieve a lot using stencils and printing.

Right: A series of separate stencils of pheasants, countryside flowers, and rabbits tells a story by being applied randomly over these cupboard doors.

Left: Cupboard doors found in a junkyard have been printed, incised, and hand painted before being aged and distressed with wax.

daisy cupboard

Stenciling a cupboard is a wonderful way to an instant kitchen transformation. Using a medieval flower stencil design of daisies, I applied it to the inside door of the cupboards. As seen here, even a detail of color and a simple design makes an enormous impact in the kitchen. Units and cupboards are the best features to decorate if you want to create an immediate transformation in your kitchen; then move onto the larger areas, such as walls, floors, and larders. Handcrafted details make the perfect, professional finish; here, I simply painted the knobs with a simple freehand design to add interest. Clean, cool colors are perfect for a peaceful look; blue and green give a fresh, clean feel, while white-based colors create a calm haven, no matter how busy your heart of the home may be.

MATERIALS

1-in. paintbrush

2-in. roller

⅛-in. paintbrush

2-in. paintbrush

Spray repositioning glue

Stencil acetate cut to size (see template, p.138–139)

Two containers for paint

25 fl. oz. wood sealer

30 fl. oz. Celadon Green chalk paint

15 fl. oz. dark blue chalk paint

15 fl. oz. Old White chalk paint

30 fl. oz. paste wax

1 Seal and paint the inside cupboard in the shade of your choice; here, I have used a pale chalk paint in Celadon Green. Use two coats and allow it to dry thoroughly. Use a ready-made stencil (see p.143 for details) or cut your stencil to size (see template on p.138–139) and affix it to the inside of the cupboard door. Spray the wrong side of the stencil with spray repositioning glue and press it onto the cupboard, making sure it is positioned straight.

2 Put the blue and white chalk paints side by side in the same paint tray, but do not mix them together. Use the 2-in. roller to lightly pick up both paints, allowing them to stay separate, and roll gently over the stencil. To allow a random effect, do not overroll or your two-tone effect will be reduced. Coat the entire stencil area with smooth strokes.

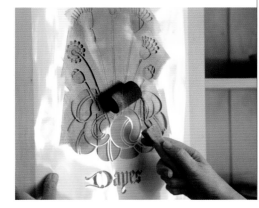

3 Peel the stencil away and allow to dry thoroughly. Wax all over and allow to dry.

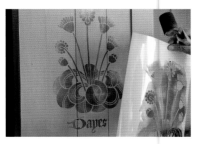

The borders of the panels have been painted in Old Ocher to act as frames. The walls of the room are painted with Mud Gray—a taupe gray color made from a mixture of purple and yellow with white.

sponged and potato printed cupboards

I decided to create this lighthearted decoration because the cupboards are a major focal point of the room. They were inspired by the naive folk art popularized by northern European furniture and the predominant style of early American settlers. The colors I used were inspired by the modern print hanging next to the cupboards by Eric Ravilious.

Each panel is long and narrow, which makes it difficult to paint a landscape on them. So I decided to divide each panel into three.

The panels have a hand-painted look, yet are worked by a technique that even someone with no confidence in drawing or painting can achieve. The technique is essentially a printing process using sponges and potatoes—tools usually allotted to young

1 Paint the panels with a background color that is deeper than the borders. Here, Plum was chosen as a base. Château Gray chalk paint was then painted by scrubbing it on with the brush to give a lightly textured effect. A little Plum shows through to give it depth. Allow to dry.

2 Tear a strip from the side of a cardboard box, then dab the straight edge generously with paint.

3 Press the painted edge of cardboard onto the panels and pull off, repeating across the width of each panel.

4 Draw a simple tree shape onto a new sponge using a marker and the template on p.140–141.

5 With a sharp pair of scissors, cut the design of the tree out, to a depth of about 1 inch.

6 Paint the sponge trees. Add extra height where necessary and make different shapes.

children. By judicious choice of colors, the result can be charming and sophisticated.

Use just a few colors that are of similar tone and shade, although one needs to be brighter than the rest to give the scene a little lift. Scaling is also very important. The design needs to be fairly bold in size. If the elements are too small, the project will not only take a long time but could also become very busy and fussy.

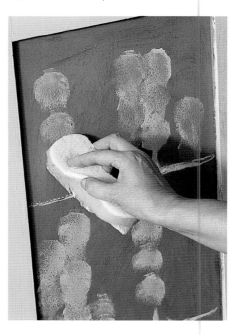

MATERIALS

30 fl. oz. Plum chalk paint

20 fl. oz. Old Ocher chalk paint

30 fl. oz. Château Gray chalk paint

10 fl. oz. each of green, Old White, and
  brown chalk paints

2-in. paintbrush

Cardboard

Marker pen

Sponge

Scissors

Potato

Roller tray

10 fl. oz. clear matte varnish

1-in. varnish brush

7 Pour white paint into a roller tray, cut a potato into a square, and use this to print the main blocks of the buildings.

8 Pour brown paint into the roller tray and use smaller potato pieces to print each window, roof, and door.

9 When dry, cover the panels and borders of the cupboard with varnish, repeating if needed.

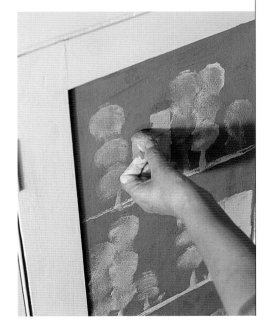

painted and incised cupboards

1 Paint the panels and allow them to dry thoroughly. These have been painted in alternative colors.

The main impact of these kitchen cupboards is the strength of the effect created by the gentle Duck Egg Blue contrasting with the pinks and teasingly showing through. Having a restrained tone as the main theme allows brighter colors to be used elsewhere in the kitchen, with plates, bowls, and other accessories picking up the pinks and blues.

This technique uses a bright color as a base that is then painted over with a milder, cooler one. While the top layer of paint is still wet, an eraser is run through it, revealing the brighter colors underneath. Remember that strong base colors generally have more impact than light ones.

This method of drawing into wet paint is much easier than trying to draw the same thing freehand. It is more like doodling, and if you do make a mistake, you can always repaint the area and draw a new shape into fresh, wet paint—taking the pressure off having to draw a perfect leaf every time.

An eraser is a soft yet firm tool to draw with, creating bold lines and preventing scratches on the surface. Always take the drawing out to the edges; it's all too easy to end up with little mean leaves in the center of the panels. This leaf pattern was inspired by an intriguing combination of Hawaiian-print shirts and Matisse drawings.

2 Cover the base coat of each panel using a neutral color, in this case Paris Gray chalk paint.

3 While still wet, draw into the paint with an eraser. Using the templates on p.136–137, start with the outline of the leaf. The paint is easy to manipulate, so you can brush over the panel if you make a mistake.

4 Incise the central and smaller veins with the eraser before painting the border.

5 Decorate the borders before varnishing. This can change the tone at first, but it soon returns to normal.

MATERIALS

10 fl. oz. pink paint

10 fl. oz. blue paint

10 fl. oz. Duck Egg Blue paint

10 fl. oz. Paris Gray paint

Eraser

1-in. paintbrush

10 fl. oz. varnish

These are old cupboards I wanted to revamp, to give a light contrast to the dark oven and to bring light into the kitchen. I decided to use just a little bright pastel to help make it lively and to match the collection of bright plates on the shelves. I like drawing into wet paint, as it is quick and beautiful in the way it reveals the color underneath. I used interesting neutrals, Duck Egg Blue, and Paris Gray to calm the bright colors.

blues
blueberries and figs

Blue is a very old and traditional color in the kitchen, partly because of the belief that it was an antiseptic and deflected flies and insects. Blue and white china has long had pride of place in the cabinets. Blue is of course a cool color, but some blues are warmer than others. The blue of the willow pattern plate is generally warm and comforting. Similarly, the Swedish gray-blues are warm and Duck Egg Blue is restful and soft. All of these work well with creams and off-whites, and with browns and beiges.

It is the antidote to food colors because there are very few foods that are blue.

Rajastan
For a powerful impact use the strong blue of Riviera Blue with creamy Linen over it.

Aztec
Like the ancient mosaics, a wash of turquoise Pacific Blue is covered with coral Ginger and shell-colored Linen.

Greek Island
The chalky intensity of Greek Blue, pale Louis Blue, and Straw.

Modern Cool
Pacific Blue with Château Gray and Urban Light are cool but colorful.

Swedish Style

For the rich tradition of painted interiors use Aubusson Blue with Château Gray and Scandinavian Pink.

Rococo

The pastel blue of Urban Light with Pink Silk counterbalanced by the caramel of Wet Clay.

Renaissance

Louis Blue is a grayish powder blue given a lift with Ginger and Riviera Blue.

Montmartre

The rich intensity of Riviera Blue is calmed with Creamy Linen and Celadon Green.

Eucalyptus

The sandy limestone brings out the green in Duck Egg Blue to make a dry, leafy, gray look.

the metallic kitchen

There has always been a lot of metal in kitchens, but using metallic finishes and decorating with them is a new idea. The days when the kitchen had only one, utilitarian look—that of a purely practical place with little in the way of decoration—are gone.

Nowadays fashion has swung to the other end of the spectrum with even the textures of the bedroom entering the kitchen, using seductive sparkles and pearly looks. There are now easy-to-use gilding materials so that applying shimmering paint or shiny materials is easy. Metallic foils, sparkle paints, and pearly luster paints are all now robust enough for the kitchen.

The traditional kitchen would have been full of copper and brass implements and fittings—from saucepans to the stoves they sat on—but the modern kitchen tends to have replaced these with a lot of stainless steel. Working with colors for the walls and units in the room to compliment the metals allows the metal to become a color in itself, again emphasizing the ability of the kitchen's functional items to become an integral part of a stylish design.

Left: The modern kitchen always contains a lot of metal, particularly stainless steel, combined with other neutral-colored materials, such as glass, slate, and wood. Combine them with cool yellows, taupes, blues, and lilacs.

inspirations

Stainless steel is probably the most commonly used metal in the modern kitchen. Being a neutral gray, it can look dull, so choosing colors that does not make it look dreary is vital.

Below: Lilacs and mauves, with a touch of ocher yellow, give this room a great contemporary look when placed alongside the neutral grays of the steel.

Opposite page: Although this room is essentially a neutral kitchen using steel as the main material, its combination with wood softens the look, as do the white-painted table legs.

Above: This is a kitchen where dramatic red makes a powerful color statement. Stainless steel is essentially gray in shadow and turns whiter under strong light. Red is used here to lift the gray and add cheer and a dash of energy; this would be an ideal setting for evening entertaining.

Right: Good lighting in potentially dark areas is especially important when working with metallic colors—as in this kitchen where the steel works well with blue cupboards and dark gray countertops.

The strong and positive colors of the black tiles and work surfaces through the rest of the room make a good, strong contrast to the copper walls. This kitchen is owned by a professional cook and is in constant use, therefore the effect needs to be bright and positive but not intrusive. The copper has only been applied to one wall and is mainly around the window, so the effect is most apparent when you first enter the kitchen.

MATERIALS

Three 2-in. paintbrushes

30 fl. oz. Lilac Slate midsheen paint

1 roll copper foil

30 fl. oz. gold size

copper-foil kitchen

Copper is a very traditional color for a kitchen, conjuring up visions of kettles and jelly molds in a rustic farmhouse. But here copper tells a very different story. Copper foil has been used on one of the walls to create an exhilarating modern effect. Used over a wall with a base of pale lilac, it's a dramatic and commanding statement for a kitchen that was originally a little bare in its coloring with black tiles under white walls.

This metallic foil, unlike conventional metal leaf, is extremely shiny and bright. As it catches the light it changes from a bright and reddish copper hue to a deeper and warmer brown. Available in many colors, it can be purchased in long rolls (see page 10 for metallic products) and is easy to apply. Before application, the copper is a thin sheet of metal bonded to a plastic sheet. The metallic side comes off the transparent plastic when rubbed onto a glue known as gold size, leaving only the sheet that is discarded. Depending on the stickiness of the size and the amount of foil you rub off, there will be more or less copper remaining on the wall.

1 Paint the wall with a base that will offer a contrast to the foil. Here Lilac Slate paint with a slight sheen was used.

3 Cut pieces of the foil so that they can be handled easily. There is a right side and a wrong side. Contrary to usual expectations, apply the sheet with the shiny metal side up.

5 Pull off the thin plastic sheeting so that all that remains is the copper. The areas where there is no copper foil will still have a layer of the sticky gold size. This should be left to lose its tackiness naturally. As the foil is not a true metal, no varnish is needed.

2 Apply gold size all over the wall. The size will at first look white, with a faint purple or blue haze. After about three or four minutes, it becomes transparent and is ready to be covered with the foil. The stickiness will gradually recede and disappear completely after several weeks.

4 Brush down with the hand or a large, strong brush. The amount of copper that comes off depends on the amount of size applied. Some walls will absorb size and so the foil will not come off so easily. If this happens, apply another layer of size before continuing. If you wear a ring, take care not to scratch the foil. The finish will not be solid and some base color will show through.

pearl kitchen

I approached this kitchen in a completely different way to the usual kitchen. I was inspired by the owner, who wanted her kitchen to be as shimmering as her collection of glittering evening dresses. I based it on a checkered, taffeta ball gown, replicating its iridescent shimmer with pearl paint in Blue, Lilac, and Green.

Pearl paint is most dramatic when painted over a dark base. The final color of the pearl paint depends on the base color, so a blue pearl will look blue over a deep blue paint but mauve over a red base. By creating a striped base that is then covered with vertical stripes of pearl paint, many other colors are made. Each pearl color covers the gray, deep blue, and deep green stripes.

Pearl paints need light to come to life, and work best if hit at an oblique angle. If the unit or wall to be painted is next to a window, ceiling lights that shine from the side and in front are needed to make the pearl paint come to life.

2 When dry, paint vertical stripes of pearl paint in Blue, Lilac, and Green. Apply the paint thinly and don't be alarmed that it appears white when first applied; it will become the appropriate color as it dries.

1 The whole unit was painted in a taupe-colored base called Mud Gray—a delightful color made from purple, yellow, and white. Over this, paint deep blue and green colored freehand bands in midsheen paint, making the edges and lines a little softer, keeping the look of fabric.

MATERIALS

30 fl. oz. Mud Gray midsheen paint
30 fl. oz. Cairo Green midsheen paint
30 fl. oz. Riviera Blue midsheen paint
10 fl. oz. Blue, Lilac, and Green pearl paint
1 roll of painting tape
Three 1-in. paintbrushes

3 To sharpen the looseness of the hand-painted stripes, put two strips of painting tape in place and paint over in blue paint.

As with anything shiny, a little goes a long way. So just the panels of this dresser have been painted with pearl paint in a checkered design. The intense, pale blue of the shelves picks up on the shining pearl alongside it.

A sophisticated kitchen cupboard has emerged from the inspiration of aging shabbiness.

This old cupboard has long been a favorite because of its useful drawers and shelves, but it was due for a fresh makeover. I have often noticed the way old metal cupboards have an attractive mixture of rusty and shiny surfaces—old metal fridges and storage cupboards all have this look. I have tried to reproduce this effect using an aluminum leaf over a rust-colored paint, before distressing the leaf with wax. The wax cuts down some of the high shine of the leaf, creating a more realistic, dulled metal look. The distressing also rubs away the leaf to reveal some of the red primer paint, which is made from the red oxide pigment that also forms rust.

To create a realistic effect when sanding down the piece, don't think of the way paint wears away, instead imagine the way rust forms. It tends to scratch and rust in spots, often helped if the underneath surface is particularly bumpy.

MATERIALS

Sandpaper

20 fl.oz. red chalk primer paint

1-in. paintbrush

10 fl.oz. gold size

Fine-haired varnish brush

1 book of aluminum leaf

30 fl.oz. clear wax

Cloth to polish and buff

Talc

silver distressed cabinet

1 Sand the cabinet. Paint a coat of red primer paint all over the cupboard and allow it to dry.

2 Take some water-based gold size (the glue for metallic leaf) and apply it only where you want the metal leaf. Do not apply too thickly or brush over it. It will be white with a faint purple tinge when it is first applied—although it dries completely clear, it will darken the paint underneath a little. The size is ready as soon as it is transparent.

3 A book of aluminum leaves will be needed—each has twenty-five leaves, approximately 5 inches square. As the leaf sticks to anything, put a little talc onto your hands to keep them dry. As soon as the leaf touches the size it will adhere, so work slowly and methodically, letting the leaf drop onto the surface without becoming too crumpled. Rub the leaf well so it adheres firmly.

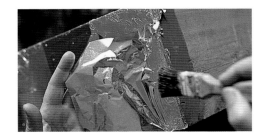

4 Take some clear wax and apply a generous amount to the surface, at first rubbing gently, and then with more force in some areas. Take a piece of sandpaper and fold it so you can make scratch marks in the leaf.

5 For final protection, apply more wax and build up the shine into a high polish.

sparkle cupboard

Bring sparkle to your kitchen! Sparkle paint can be easily applied to cupboards and units to give them a dazzling allure. The paint is a clear varnish embedded with tiny pieces of glitter. Although available in Blue, Green, and Red, the finished effect depends on the base color. For example, if Green sparkle paint is painted on pink, its green glitter will appear to be in the pink base. The sparkle paint is most successful when it combines with deeper or brighter base colors, so the sparkles have more tones to react with.

1 Paint the base in a dark blue water-based paint, or another color of your choice that is strong or bright, and allow it to dry. Apply a coat of the sparkle paint. It will look white at first, but it will dry clear.

MATERIALS

20 fl. oz. Riviera Blue paint

15 fl. oz. Green sparkle paint

Two 1-in. paintbrushes

Several layers of Green sparkle paint were applied over Riviera Blue paint to give this small cupboard a new life and vigor. A line of green was used along the scalloped edge, a shiny new glass knob was used, and the old cupboard has a place in a bright and colorful kitchen.

The sparkle finish tends not to spread evenly, giving it a delightful look, reminiscent of a starlit night. The finish will not be completely even because the glitter is dispersed through the varnish and the brush does not spread it uniformly.

2 For extra sparkles apply a second coat over the first.

3 If necessary, paint a third coat, possibly in a different sparkle paint. Be extra careful washing the brush, since the sparkles have a tendency to stick to the brush.

metallics
stainless steel, copper, brass, and pearl

We are used to using metals for the appliances and work surfaces, such as stainless steel and copper, but not on the cupboards or walls.

We have added other shiny finishes, like pearl and sparkle, to the usual metal finishes of brass, gold, copper, aluminum, and silver. The colors and textures of the bedroom are entering the kitchen as we add alluring and seductive colors and silky textures.

The metallics need to be matched with a little color to set them off, such as green or blue with copper and bright pink with the gold. Pearls and sparkles can luxuriate with strong pastels and bright colors.

Georgian Inspiration
Deep muted Château Gray and Old White over brass gold leaf suggest the eighteenth century.

Art Nouveau
Silver Foil with Linen over a base of Lilac Slate recalls Charles Rennie Mackintosh.

Italian Palazzo

Primer Red, the base of much painted furniture, is used here with distressed Brass Gold Leaf and Château Gray.

Verdigris

Copper Leaf distressed to show the Château Gray wash beneath with the Celadon Green.

Persian Palace

Rich Persian Green, used with a touch of Celadon Green and the splendor of the Copper Foil.

Pearly Passion

Mud Gray, a warm, midtone taupe, is the base for Lilac, Blue, and Green pearl paint.

Silver Filigree

The warm saturated Greek Blue works as a perfect foil for the Silver Foil.

Powerful Pink

Hawaiian Pink is a vivacious color, perfect for reflecting the bright Gold Foil and the Lilac Pearl.

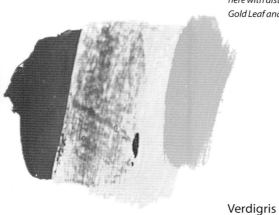

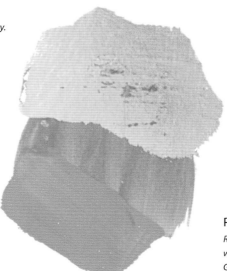

templates

USING TEMPLATES

Templates are supplied for the Sponged
and Potato-printed Cupboards (see p.114)
and the Painted and Incised Cupboards
(see p.118) as well as a series of Leaf and
Flower designs I have created for you to use
in other wall and cupboard projects, or as a
variation on the Daisy Cupboard (see
p. 112). You can use the template designs
on these pages as a basis for hand-painted
or traced designs. For freehand work,
simply copy the design on to the piece you
wish to paint in pencil, then, once you are
happy with the design, trace over it in a
thicker pencil line. To use as a template,
photocopy the relevant design, enlarging if
necessary, and transfer the design to
transfer or tracing paper using a thick,
black pen. Trace on to your surface using
thick pencil line.

*Painted and Incised Cupboards
(see p.118)*

*Painted and Incised Cupboards,
variations (see p.118)*

*Daisy Cupboard, variations
(see p.112). See p.143 for details
of the ready-made stencil used
in the project.*

Rose

Oak Leaf

Leaves and seeds

Bouquet

Marguerite

MAKING STENCILS FROM TEMPLATES

Use these designs as stencils by photocopying and enlarging the designs to fit the size of your furniture. Once you have decided on the size of your stencil, buy an acetate sheet large enough to fit over the stencil with a generous overlap. Placing the stencil photocopy over the acetate, and fix it in place with tape over a self-healing cutting mat. Now cut it out carefully, using a sharp craft knife, always working away from you. Cut from the center outward, and fix any breaks or tears with slivers of masking tape, cutting the shape again in the masking tape. If you are using a hot cutting knife or a heatpen, use a sheet of glass as a base. To use a stencil on walls or furniture, secure it to the surface with spray glue.

*Sponged and Potato-
printed Cupboards
(see p.114)*

suppliers

Annie Sloan Practical Style
117 London Road
Headington UK OX3 9HZ
Tel: +44 (0) 1865 768666
e-mail:
paint@anniesloan.com
Annie Sloan paints and
products are online at:
www.anniesloan.com

PAINT USA
US Distributor of Annie
    Sloan paints:
Details Home Concept
    Gallery
342 West Market St.
York, PA 17401
Tel: 717 840 7919

Tallgrass
Home Expressions Studio
370 West Market St.
York, PA 17401
Tel: 717 840 7919

Ace Hardware
2200 Kensington Ct.
Oak Brook, IL 60523-2100
Tel: 630 990 6600
www.acehardware.com

Adco Paint & Supply Co.
1933 East McDowell Street
Phoenix, AZ
Tel: 602 253 8471

Adelaide's Paint & Decor
101 Palmetto Street
St Simons Island, GA 31522
Tel: 912 634 1406

Adler Brothers Inc.
173 Wickenden Street
Providence, RI 02903
Tel: 401 421 5157

Ameritone
140 Alamaha Street
Kahului, HI 86732
Tel: 808 871 7734

Ann Arbor Paint
2386 West Stadium
    Boulevard
Ann Arbor, MI 48103
Tel: 734 662 6690

Andrew Inc.
2310 East Douglas Street
Wichita, KS 67214
Tel: 316 267 3328

Babel's Paint & Decorating
692 Pleasant Street Rear
Norwood, MA 02062
Tel: 781 762 3128

Bankston's Paint Center
856 Division Street
Biloxi, MS 39530
Tel: 228 374 8807

Benjamin Moore & Co.
51 Chestnut Ridge Road
Montvale, NJ 07645
Tel: 800 344 0400
www.benjaminmoore.com

Boone Paint & Interiors
1852 NC Hwy 105 South
Boone, NC 28607
Tel: 828 264 9220

Budeke's
418 South Broadway
Baltimore, MD 21231
Tel: 410 732 4354

Creative Paint & Decorating
107 S. Second Street
Boonville, IN 47601
Tel: 812 897 4268

Curtis & Campbell Inc.
6239 B Street #102
Anchorage, AK 99518
Tel: 907 561 6011

Dove Brushes & Tools
1849 Oakmont Avenue
Tarpon Springs, FL 34689
Tel: 800 334 DOVE
Fax: 727 934 1142
www.dovebrushes.com

Gragg's Paint Co.
275 Southwest Boulevard
Kansas City, KS 66103
Tel: 913 432 8818

Grand Strand Paint & Supply
11530 #1 Hwy 17 Bypass
Murrells Inlet, SC 29576
Tel: 843 651 8572

Helm Paint
8130 Earhart Boulevard
New Orleans, LA 70118
Tel: 504 861 8179

Hirshfield's
725 Second Avenue North
Minneapolis, MN 55406
Tel: 612 377 3910

Home Depot
2455 Paces Ferry Road
Atlanta, GA 30339
Tel: 800 430 3376
www.homedepot.com

Janovic Plaza
30–35 Thomson Avenue
Long Island City, NY 11101
Tel: 718 392 3999

JC Licht
45 N. Brandon Drive
Glendale Heights, IL 60139
Tel: 630 351 0400

Lowe's Home Improvement
    Warehouse
P.O. Box 1111
North Wilkesboro, NC 28656
Tel: 800 44LOWES
www.lowes.com

Mark's Paint
4830 Vineland Avenue
North Hollywood, CA 91601
Tel: 818 766 3949

Memorial Paint & Decorating
14049 Memorial Drive
Houston, TX 77079
Tel: 281 496 2082

Monarch Paint
5608 Connecticut Avenue NW
Washington, DC 20015
Tel: 301 587 2166

Mountaintop Mosaic
P.O. Box 653
Castleton, VT 05735-0653
Tel: 800 564 4980
mountaintopmosaics.com

O-Gee Paint Company
6995 Bird Road
Miami, FL 33155
Tel: 305 666 3300

Old City Paint
210 West Girard Avenue
Philadelphia, PA 19123
Tel: 215 625 8300

Smith & Hawken
Tel: 800 940 1170
www.smithandhawken.com

PAINT UK
Bailey's Paint
Griffin Mill Estate
London Rd.
New Stroud, Thrupp
Glos GL5 2AZ
Tel: +44 (0)1453 882237

Interior Affairs
Decorative Furniture,
Painting and Accessories
6 The Grove
Westbourne
Emsworth
Hampshire PO10 8UJ
Tel: +44 (0)1243 389972

Creative Decorating
Decorative Furniture,
Painting and Accessories
Maranatha, Whitbrock
Wadebridge, Cornwall
PL27 7ED
Tel: +44 (0)1208 814528

STENCILS
The stencil for the Daisy
Cupboard on page 112 was
obtained from the
Stencil Library (stencil: Daisy,
GMT 92). You can order
stencils and stenciling
equipment online from
www.anniesloan.com or
direct from The Stencil
Library website below.

The Stencil Library
Stocksfield Hall
Stocksfield
Northumberland
NE43 7TN
United Kingdom
Tel: +44 (0) 1661 844 844
Fax: +44 (0) 1661 843 984
Email: info@stencil-library.com
www.stencil-library.com

acknowledgments

All the paints and products used in this book are Annie Sloan Paints and products. I am very grateful to Nicky Anderton, Alison Eden, Meg Macmillan, Angela Palmer, and Lalla Ward who allowed us to photograph their kitchens, and in particular Sue and Douglas Ronald who allowed us almost to take over their house and cottage. I also want to thank Claire Cairns, and Ashley and Sarah Goodall who were brave enough to allow us to photograph their kitchen while I decorated the walls. Some of the work was carried out by Annie Sloan Practical Style's team of designers including Jo Hewanicka, Interior Designer (Tel: +44 (0) 1865 875690; Email: josiahewanicka@ globalnet.co.uk) and Kelly Fannon.

I am also very appreciative of Claudia Easom, Interior Decorator (Tel: +44 (0)1865 469042/+44 (0) 7986 676283) for her white French kitchen, and stylist Hilary Monson (Tel: +44 (0)1993 852440), for her African kitchen. I would also like to thank AllWood, Oxford, for their help.

I would like to thank Cindy, Georgina, Robin, and Tino for being just brilliant! Lastly I want to say a deep thank you to David, Henry, Felix, and Hugo Manuel for all their help in the shop, on the web site, and mostly at home.

picture credits

The publishers would like to thank Tino Tedaldi for the photography in this book, except for the photographs mentioned below:
Page 34, top © Neil Davis/Elizabeth Whiting
Page 34, bottom © Nick Carter/Elizabeth Whiting
Page 35 © Huntley Hedworth/Elizabeth Whiting
Page 49, left © David Markham/Elizabeth Whiting
Page 68, top left © Red Cover/Jake Fitzjones
Page 68, top middle © Red Cover/Jake Fitzjones
Page 68, bottom left © Red Cover/Jake Fitzjones
Page 68, bottom right © Rodney Hyett/Elizabeth Whiting
Page 85 © Lu Jeffery/Elizabeth Whiting
Page 109 © Di Lewis/Elizabeth Whiting
Page 110 © Andreas von Einsiedel/Elizabeth Whiting
Page 111, top left © Ian Perry/Elizabeth Whiting
Page 111, bottom right © Dennis Stone/Elizabeth Whiting
Page 122 © Michael Crockett/Elizabeth Whiting
Page 124, top right © Red Cover/Jake Fitzjones
Page 124, bottom left © Red Cover/Henry Wilson
Page 124, bottom right © Red Cover/Guglielmo Galvin
Page 125 © Red Cover/Jake Fitzjones

index